BARNS, BARBECUE and BALES of COTTON
A RURAL RETROSPECTIVE OF SOUTH CAROLINA AGRICULTURE

Clemson University's College of Agriculture, Forestry and Life Sciences

The mission of Clemson University's College of Agriculture, Forestry and Life Sciences, consistent with our land grant university role, is to provide teaching, research and service in agriculture, forestry and life sciences that will benefit the citizens of South Carolina and the nation. The College of Agriculture, Forestry and Life Sciences serves more than 2,700 graduate and undergraduate students.

South Carolina Farm Bureau Federation

The mission of the South Carolina Farm Bureau Federation is to promote agricultural interests in the state of South Carolina and to optimize the lives of those involved in agriculture, while being respectful to the needs and concerns of all citizens in our state. Farm Bureau's objectives are concentrated in three key areas: education, legislation and organization.

THE DONNING COMPANY
PUBLISHERS

My parents, Blain and Nelle Player, in a sunflower field on their beloved Pondville Farms in Bishopville, South Carolina, on Highway 154 in lovely Lee County.

DEDICATION

In loving memory of my father, Cleland Blain Player Jr. (1925–2007), who passed away during the production of *Barns, Barbecue and Bales of Cotton*. He was a proud South Carolinian who lived a meaningful life as a son, brother, husband, father, uncle, grandfather and friend; as a farmer, conservationist, outdoorsman and rural leader; as a Clemson Agricultural and Mechanical College graduate, a Golden Tiger alumnus and a Tiger sports fan; as a brave United States Marine; and as a loyal, joyful man of the Christian faith. He was—and is—my greatest hero!

And in honor of my mother, Nelle Kirby Player, whose love, support, discipline, instruction and friendship shaped me into the person I am today. She has been an exemplary farmwife, homemaker and community leader; a wise teacher and a loving mother; and a gracious and hospitable hostess, who has served up more home-cooked meals of barbecue and similar Southern delicacies than can be counted. She inspires me every day.

Copyright © 2010 by the Clemson University College of Agriculture, Forestry and Life Sciences

All rights reserved, including the right to reproduce this work in any form whatsoever without permission in writing from the publisher, except for brief passages in connection with a review. For information, please write:

The Donning Company Publishers
184 Business Park Drive, Suite 206
Virginia Beach, VA 23462

Steve Mull, General Manager
Barbara Buchanan, Office Manager
Heather L. Floyd, Editor
Lori Wiley, Graphic Designer
Derek Eley, Imaging Artist
Lori Kennedy, Project Research Coordinator
Tonya Hannink, Marketing Specialist
Pamela Engelhard, Marketing Advisor

Bernie and Lynn Walton, Project Directors

Cataloging-in-Publication Data
Barns, barbecue, and bales of cotton : a rural retrospective of South Carolina agriculture / edited by W. Kirby Player ; foreword by Walter Edgar ; with contributions by Robert A. Graham, Lake E. High, Jr., Rowland P. Alston, Jr.
       p. cm.
   Includes bibliographical references.
   ISBN 978-1-57864-589-3 (hardcover : alk. paper)
   1. Agriculture--South Carolina--History. 2. Farm life--South Carolina--History. 3. Agriculture--South Carolina--Pictorial works. 4. Farm life--South Carolina--Pictorial works. 5. Farm buildings--South Carolina--Pictorial works. 6. South Carolina--Economic conditions. 7. South Carolina--Social life and customs. 8. South Carolina--Pictorial works. 9. Agriculture--South Carolina--Societies, etc. I. Player, W. Kirby, 1961- II. Graham, Robert A. III. High, Lake E. IV. Alston, Rowland P.
   S451.S7B37 2010
   630.9757--dc22
                            2009042316

Printed in the United States of America at Walsworth Publishing Company

TABLE OF CONTENTS

7   Foreword

11   Preface

15   Acknowledgments

19   Introduction

23   Barns—Icons of Agriculture
         The Lowcountry
         The Pee Dee
         The Piedmont
         The Upstate
         The Barns of Clemson University
         Working Buildings, Equipment and Life on the Farm

93   Barbecue—The Taste, Fellowship and Fun of South Carolina

113   Bales of Cotton—The Products of South Carolina Agriculture
         Beef Cattle
         Corn
         Cotton
         Dairy
         Ornamental Horticulture and the Green Industry
         Peaches
         Poultry
         Soybeans
         Tobacco
         Other Commodities

139   State and National Organizations
         Clemson University College of Agriculture, Forestry and Life
            Sciences
         South Carolina Farm Bureau Federation
         South Carolina Department of Agriculture
         United States Department of Agriculture Natural Resources
            Conservation Service
         National FFA Organization
         South Carolina 4-H Youth Development Program

153   The Future of Agriculture

158   Resource Guide

159   About the Contributors

Five tobacco stick barns stand in a row in Horry County. Such tobacco stick barns were once a common sight in South Carolina. Photograph courtesy of NASS.

FOREWORD

For more than forty years I have researched and written about the wonderful, rich history of South Carolina. Like many historians of an earlier century, I have frequently taken roads less traveled to get the lay of the land—from the Lowcountry with its abandoned rice fields and prosperous truck farms, to the Pee Dee and Midlands with their rich acres of tobacco and cotton, to the rolling hills of the Upcountry with its peach orchards. Everywhere, there were forests—where once crops were raised. And, along with the changing rural landscape of our state, there stand visible reminders of the role agriculture has played—and continues to play—in our economy and our history.

South Carolinians cherish our past and the visible reminders of our state's rich heritage. Today, we refer to those cherished images as icons, and like the older meaning of the word, these images can be sources of inspiration. The best-known of our state's icons is the state tree, the Sabal Palmetto. I chose it as the cover for my book *South Carolina: A History* because to me it embraces and expresses in one potent symbol the very essence of the Palmetto State.

Through my research and travels, I believe that there are other iconic symbols of South Carolina—especially of our agricultural past. For the first three centuries of our existence as a colony and a state, agriculture was the economic endeavor that involved the overwhelming majority of our people. And nothing speaks to the tradition and heritage of agriculture better than barns, bales of cotton and barbecue.

Barns and other outbuildings have been a part of the built landscape of our state for literally centuries. They speak to the centrality of farming in all its many forms. It was not unusual for barns and other related farm buildings to be more impressive structures than the homes of those who tilled the land. In driving the back roads of South Carolina, there are few images more evocative to me than barns—whether it is one still in use or, sadly, a dilapidated, abandoned one. Some of those barns might have held cotton.

Today, if one were to ask an individual anywhere in the country what he or she associates with South Carolina agriculture, the answer would inevitably be "cotton." Although Carolinians have been growing a variety of crops since 1670, South Carolina was the first cotton-producing state. From 1790 until 1820, it was also the leading cotton-producing state in the nation, and after the Civil War the state's farmers abandoned virtually every other crop to plant cotton.

In addition to cotton, South Carolinians learned to enjoy nature's bounty in the form of barbecue. The state is home to more varieties of barbecue than any other state. There are seventeenth-century references to the term "barbecue." Then and now, the making of barbecue is a community event. It is an ingrained cultural tradition that crosses regional boundaries within the state. While proponents of Pee Dee (pepper and vinegar), mustard, tomato and ketchup versions of barbecue tout theirs as the best, it can be said that *all* South Carolina barbecue is good! And it should be remembered that in the Palmetto State, barbecue is a noun—not a verb.

These three icons are powerful images of our state's agricultural traditions. Barns are symbols of the clearing of the wilderness and storehouses of nature's bounty drawn from tilling the soil. Barbecue speaks to the enjoyment of nature's bounty in the company of family, friends and neighbors. Cotton is representative of the many and varied agricultural commodities cultivated in South Carolina over the centuries.

Within the pages of this book, you will discover through photographs and words the weaving together of a narrative that creates an understanding that the connectivity of rural life and agriculture is essential to an understanding of our state's history, economy and culture. This project, like virtually every occurrence in a traditional agricultural society, has been a community effort. Many, many South Carolinians—from rural back roads to burgeoning urban centers—have contributed images and historical information. Together, they tell at least part of the story of agriculture in South Carolina, a story that stretches from the sea islands that front the Atlantic Ocean to the foothills of the Appalachian Mountains.

Unfortunately, some of the subjects depicted in these pages have disappeared. One of the well-documented traditions of South Carolina agriculture—especially in the years prior to 1860—was a willingness to adopt new crops and methods and abandon those that no longer were profitable. One of the best contemporary examples is the disappearance of tobacco barns in the Pee Dee. Not so long ago, I could drive from Columbia to Conway and see along the way log, tarpaper, wooden shake, and brick barns. Now, barns are rare, replaced by metal containers.

Some may find these changes disheartening, but their original construction and their later disappearance speak to the changing nature of agriculture. Remember, no matter where you are, you only have to drive a short distance to glimpse South Carolina's scenic rural vistas or to savor some true Southern comfort food. Remember, *all* South Carolina barbecue is good!

Walter Edgar

Bright white cotton against a vivid blue sky. Photograph by Larry Kemmerlin, South Carolina Farm Bureau Federation.

The Horton family operated Horton's Mill, located on Highway 151 just north of McBee, for at least seventy-five years. Its sign advertises "Fresh Meal Grits Ground Daily." The current status is not known. Photograph and information contributed by Walter K. Lewis Jr.

PREFACE

Anyone driving along the highways and byways of South Carolina, especially the winding farm-to-market back roads of our beautiful state, cannot help but notice the barns and farm buildings that still grace the changing countryside. Each of these monuments stands as a testimony to the industry and economic strength of rural South Carolina. These buildings exist in various states and conditions. Some are weathered and aging but still provide shelter and storage for their users, while others have enjoyed complete renovation, restoration or thoughtful replacement with their more modern cousins. Others show the obvious signs of abandonment, having been claimed by grasping vines like kudzu or wisteria. Still others have fallen victim to progress—part of a lovely farmstead standing strong one week, only to disappear the next, as yet another new development sprawls into the countryside. South Carolina is in a cycle of population growth and economic and cultural change. With this movement there is a noticeable decline in the pastoral scenes that have crowned our rural lands for many years. It is this recognition that spurred the creation of this book.

Whatever the state or style of these hardy structures, there is no denying that there is magic and mystery in old barns and farm structures. These rural sentinels, from a distant view and especially upon close inspection, are marvels of rural architecture—genuine treasures of form, function and farm life. These buildings are more than wood, metal and various other building materials. Many were and are the symbolic heart and soul of rural agricultural production in South Carolina. They provide shelter from the elements and storage for equipment, crops and livestock. They also act as billboards for the families of each farm, proclaiming to all who pass by, "We work with the land and all of creation to provide food and fiber for ourselves and others!"

And what of the activities of the farm and the family? This book seeks not only to capture the beauty and wonder of South Carolina's barns, but also the life, productivity and fellowship that exist within and around them. What crops and livestock have found their homes in or passed through the portals of these farm structures? What forms of fun and fellowship have South Carolinians shared beneath the tin roof of a tobacco barn? How many generations have rested in the shade of an old oak tree next to a hay barn? These questions are explored and brought to life in the barbecue and bales of cotton portions of this book. Barbecue is representative of rural family fun and fellowship and the joy of coming together around the table to spend time with loved ones. Cotton is but one of South Carolina's agricultural commodities, and represents all the crops and commodities that drive the agricultural economy in the state.

Agribusiness represents the largest economic engine among South Carolina's industrial sectors, contributing $34 billion to the economy each year and creating more than 200,000 jobs. Farmers use computers, satellite technology and robotics to produce the safest, most abundant and most affordable source of food, fiber and fuel in the world. Yet there remains a deep-seated nostalgia to our memories of an agrarian society.

With the creation of *Barns, Barbecue and Bales of Cotton: A Rural Retrospective of South Carolina*, we hope to stir nostalgia in those who have played a part in South Carolina's agricultural heritage so they'll be compelled to share their treasured memories with younger generations. For those who are fully engaged as agriculturalists today and often wonder about the future of rural South Carolina, we want to honor their efforts and encourage hope. There is a bright future for rural South Carolina and for the people who still till and keep the land. That future will be different than what many have known, but it will be strong. For just as some of the barns pictured in this book have stood strong through wave after wave of change, so too will the traditions and trends of our state. The old will blend with the new. We will adapt. Those of us who love the land and all that rural life represents will continue to be a part of South Carolina's future landscape. We will continue to enjoy the sights, sounds, smells and flavors of barns, barbecue and bales of cotton.

David M. Winkles Jr., President
South Carolina Farm Bureau Federation

Autumn leaves frame a wooden pole barn in southern Bamberg County. Photograph and information contributed by Minnie Miller.

The objective of the Environmental and Natural Resources curriculum at Clemson University is to produce professionals who have a broad-based knowledge in natural resources and the ability to interact with other resource professionals to provide thoughtful solutions to environmental and natural resource problems. Students get plenty of field experience.

ACKNOWLEDGMENTS

The production and publication of this book was a group effort if ever there was one. Without the help and devotion of a very long list of people, it would not—could not—have been possible. I am grateful to each of the people acknowledged here for the vital and meaningful part they played in making this project a success. The sale of this book will raise money to fund much-needed agricultural scholarships for students and to meet other academic needs in the areas of agricultural education. This is the main purpose behind its creation. But it is also a personally meaningful project for me, one that is dear to my heart. I come from a rural farming family and my work at Clemson University continues to further the success of our state's agricultural industry. It means a great deal to me that each person listed here gave of his or her time, talent, resources or finances to make this book possible.

I would like to thank the following:

The South Carolina Farm Bureau Foundation. Without its financial support, this book would not have been possible. In particular, the support, patience and grace of Larry McKenzie and Reggie Hall was vital.

The citizens of South Carolina, who shared their photographs and stories. This book is intended to honor and celebrate you and your families and the contribution you have each made to our great state.

Marilyn Pilgrim Player, my loving wife, best friend and head cheerleader.

The Office of the Dean of the College of Agriculture, Forestry and Life Sciences at Clemson University. Three deans have graciously shepherded me in this project—former deans Dr. Calvin Schoulties and Dr. Alan Sams, and current interim dean Dr. Thomas Scott. The Dean's Office support staff and the "Circle of Life" team in the office have been vital in allowing me to produce this book. Without their patience and encouragement, it would not have come to fruition.

Shannon Lee Clark, project editorial coordinator. Shannon was God's special gift to me to ensure this project was completed with professionalism and quality.

Thanks and appreciation are also offered to the following individuals and organizations:

Rowland P. Alston Jr., Clemson University Extension agent emeritus and host of the South Carolina ETV Network program *Making it Grow!*, for his contributions to the text of this book and his positive impact on agriculture in South Carolina.

Dr. Walter B. Edgar, professor of history at the University of South Carolina and official South Carolina Barbeque Association certified judge. Dr. Edgar graciously authored this book's foreword and was an avid supporter of the project from its infancy.

Robert A. Graham, former director of the South Carolina Field Office of the National Agricultural Statistics Service of the United States Department of Agriculture. I consider him to be the father of this publication—it was his idea to collect photographs of barns in South Carolina that launched this project. Many of the photos he collected are featured in this book, having been secured by Mr. Graham for inclusion.

Lake E. High Jr., president of the South Carolina Barbeque Association. He contributed his expertise to this book and has long served as an "evangelist" for South Carolina barbecue. His personality is as flavorful as the best barbecue plate in South Carolina.

The Alumni Board of the College of Agriculture, Forestry and Life Sciences at Clemson University. This group of volunteers, whose devotion to the industries of agriculture and natural resources, as well as Clemson University, inspires me every day, has my heartfelt gratitude. I offer specific thanks to the following board members: John Parris, who had the initial idea for this book and was a contributor, and Bert Bagley, Beth Crocker and Aaron Wood, for their assistance with numerous tasks related to this book's production.

Trent Allen, owner and operator of Allen's Creations in Clemson, South Carolina, contributor.

Rhonda Brandt, United States Department of Agriculture–National Agricultural Statistics Service, director, South Carolina Field Office, contributor.

Barbara Tener Clark, contributor.

The Clemson University Extension agents and Agricultural Education instructors who gathered information.

Tommy Coleman, retired tobacco specialist, Pee Dee Research and Education Center, contributor, tobacco commodities.

Janson Cox, director, South Carolina Cotton Museum, consultant.

Michaele Duke, photographer.

Douglas Edgeworth, photographer.

Edible Lowcountry magazine.

Donna Foster, executive director, South Carolina Nursery and Landscape Association, contributor, horticulture commodities.

Dewitt Gooden, research associate, Pee Dee Research and Education Center, contributor, tobacco commodities.

Fred Holder, contributor.

Sennah Honea, who has been the wind beneath my wings on the job for twenty years.

Marie Johns, South Carolina Field Office of the United States Department of Agriculture's National Agricultural Statistics Service, contributor.

Larry Kemmerlin, Promotion and Education Division, South Carolina Farm Bureau Federation, photographer.

Dr. Desmond R. Layne, Department of Horticulture, Clemson University, contributor, peach commodities.

Amy Maxwell, United States Department of Agriculture's Natural Resources Conservation Service, state public affairs specialist, contributor and promoter.

Amy S. McCune, state 4-H events coordinator, Clemson University Extension, contributor.

Philip R. Perry, Saluda County Clemson University Extension agent, contributor, dairy commodities.

Dr. Jerome V. Reel Jr., Clemson University historian, contributor.

Brian Roberts, photographer.

Saddler Taylor, contributor.

Becky Walton, director of Communications and Public Information, South Carolina Department of Agriculture and contributor, for her ideas, suggestions and sympathies throughout this process.

Bernie and Lynn Walton, my patient and supportive representatives from Donning Company Publishers.

The Honorable Hugh Weathers, South Carolina commissioner of agriculture.

David M. Winkles Jr., president, South Carolina Farm Bureau Federation, contributor.

Aaron Wood, executive director, South Carolina Soybean Association, contributor, soybean commodities.

Pat Wright, photographer.

J. K. York, photographer. Mr. York is a professional photographer who allowed his work to be published in this book at no charge. His work can be viewed at www.redbubble.com/people/jkyork.

W. Kirby Player, Editor

Miss Rachael Tinsley with some of the peaches grown on the John Tinsley farm in Spartanburg, South Carolina, 1938.

INTRODUCTION

The Alumni Board of the College of Agriculture, Forestry and Life Sciences (CAFLS) at Clemson University continually searches for ways to preserve and promote the agriculture and natural resources industries to the people of South Carolina. Its motivation stems from the vision cast by Thomas Green Clemson nearly 125 years ago as he sought to provide a "high seminary of learning" for the agricultural and mechanical arts—a vision that remains foundational to Clemson University and that has, in large part, been responsible for the success these industries have enjoyed in the entire state of South Carolina.

Nearly six years ago, Mr. John Parris, a charter member of the Alumni Board, suggested that a pictorial history of rural South Carolina and its agricultural heritage be compiled. One of the main reasons for his suggestion was the recognition that many of the men and women who experienced and contributed to some of the most significant cultural and technological transformations in South Carolina's agricultural history were passing on. A book such as this one would chronicle the state's rich agricultural heritage as well as honor these individuals who, through their hard work, sacrifice and perseverance, made South Carolina the agricultural leader it is today. The idea began to take shape as the board sought ways to supplement its scholarship endowments, and contact was made with a publisher that specialized in producing this particular type of book.

After nearly two years of seeking support and funding for the project, a serendipitous meeting occurred between the executive director of the CAFLS Alumni Board and the now retired director of the South Carolina Office of the National Agricultural Statistics Service (NASS), Mr. Bob Graham. Mr. Graham and his staff had been photographing barns and collecting barn pictures from the general public throughout South Carolina in an effort to preserve history and generate a photo essay for their annual report. The agency approved the utilization of these photos for a "barn book" and the project gained momentum. The South Carolina Farm Bureau Foundation then agreed to become a funding sponsor for the book in order to raise funds for its youth agriculture programs and scholarships through book sales.

With both NASS and the South Carolina Farm Bureau committed to the project, the Alumni Board granted approval. The publisher was secured and photo collection began. Given the broad nature and vast impact of all that is "rural South Carolina," it was also decided that the book would explore the social and familial aspects of rural South Carolina, as

Clemson University student Jason Muise captured the old dairy barn just after an early March snowfall blanketed the campus in 2009. Copyright Jason Muise Photography 2009.

well as the state's agricultural commodities and resources, represented by the barbecue and bales of cotton sections, respectively.

Photographs were accepted from the public for nearly a year and a half. The editors received some 1,200 photographs, including those provided by the NASS from its archives. Not all the photographs that were received met the submission guidelines, but it was encouraging and inspiring to observe the pride and love South Carolina's citizens have for its rural heritage. The greatest challenge was selecting which photographs to include in this book. Our preference would have been to include all the submissions; however, limited space, original and reproduction quality of the photographs and adherence to the stated themes of the book limited the editors in their selections, and only a small portion of those submitted were chosen for inclusion. We would like to extend a hearty thanks to everyone who took the time to share his or her photographs. We honor you and the part you have played in South Carolina's agricultural and rural tradition.

It is our sincere hope that the iconic images and engaging editorial copy contained in *Barns, Barbecue and Bales of Cotton* will inspire and capture all who read it. Perhaps older readers will proudly and fondly reminisce as they turn the pages and reflect on their contribution to South Carolina's rural history. Hopefully, some younger readers will be motivated to consider choosing a career in an agricultural, natural resources or related field. For those engaged in areas of work or life that are neither rural nor agricultural, perhaps this book will provide you with an understanding of how vital and essential agriculture is to South Carolina's economy and people, and what a rich legacy it possesses in the Palmetto State. And finally, it is our intention that this book and the funds it generates will go a long way in protecting the past while promoting the future of agriculture and rural life in South Carolina.

W. Kirby Player, Editor

This Greenville County barn, with its bright red paint and white trim, is an example of what many people would label the quintessential barn. Photograph courtesy of NASS.

BARNS—ICONS OF AGRICULTURE
By Robert A. Graham

Barns. They house tractors and plows, hay and tobacco, cows, horses… even kittens. They are vital to any farm. But what else? What more? What can we discover when we pause to really consider—to genuinely *see*—South Carolina's barns? What story do they tell?

Barns are rural libraries, filled with years of memories, both sad and sweet. Oh, if their walls could speak. A young boy bursting with pride as he stacks his first wagonload of hay and then unloads the bales in the haymow of his grandpa's barn. A little girl watching wide-eyed as her daddy demonstrates how to milk the cows. A husband and wife dancing cheek to cheek as the sun sets over an annual barn dance. Wrestling in the hay… grooming the horses… discussing the harvest… lamenting the drought… there are as many memories as there are nooks and crannies in the barn itself.

Barns stand as monuments to rural South Carolina, each one a testimony to the state's rich agricultural history. The aroma of drying tobacco. The warmth of the livestock on a cold winter's morning. The *cock-a-doodle-doo* of a rooster ushering in the day. Near perfect rows of wheat and corn bathed in the golden afternoon sun. Wispy bales of cotton piled high. Fresh, juicy fruits and vegetables in the brightest of colors. Barns play a central role in the production of every one of the state's agricultural commodities. They are symbolic of the hard work and perseverance of those who owned and worked the land. And those who still do.

There are many barn lovers throughout South Carolina. For some, their love and appreciation of barns began at birth—they were born into families whose members have worked the state's farmland for as long as anyone can remember and the family barn has always been the center of life and livelihood. For others, their affection for the state's barns came later in life or developed over time. Perhaps they came to appreciate these iconic structures as they drove along the state's roads. Maybe in their escape from hectic city life, they landed in rural South Carolina and inherited a beautiful barn when they purchased property.

Regardless of when the fondness of barns came, there is no question that the barns of South Carolina comfort us and hearten us. They remind us of who we are and inspire us to be all that we can be. They evoke fond memories of the past, and they motivate us to continue working for the future. They represent the agricultural history of South Carolina. They epitomize the times of hard work and the times of sweet rest; the richer times and the poorer times; and the hopes and dreams, successes and

PROP US UP ON OUR LEANIN' SIDE

Every time I pray, I think of the old deacon who always prayed, "Lord, prop us up on our leanin' side."

After hearing him pray that prayer many times, someone asked him why he prayed that prayer so fervently.

He answered, "Well sir, you see, it's like this: I got an old barn out back. It's been there a long time, it's withstood a lot of weather, it's gone through a lot of storms, and it's stood for many years. It's still standing, but one day I noticed it was leanin' to one side a bit. So I went and got some pine poles and propped it up on its leanin' side so it wouldn't fall.

"Then I got to thinking 'bout that and how much I was like that old barn. I've been around a long time, I've withstood a lot of life's storms, I've withstood a lot of bad weather in life, I've withstood a lot of hard times, and I'm still standing too.

"But I find myself leanin' to one side from time to time, so I like to ask the Lord to prop us up on our leanin' side, 'cause I figure a lot of us get to leanin' at times. Sometime we get to leanin' toward anger, leanin' toward bitterness, leanin' toward hatred, leanin' toward cussing, leanin' toward a lot of things that we shouldn't. So we need to pray, 'Lord, prop us up on our leanin' side,' so we will stand straight and tall again to glorify the Lord."

Author Unknown

struggles, celebrations and losses of those who work the land. Our barns and all that they represent are central to South Carolina's past, present and future.

South Carolina is fortunate, indeed privileged, to have a considerable number of old, historic barns and farm working buildings still standing in its fields and meadows. Even so, they seem to be disappearing from our landscape at an alarming rate, and many exist only in faded photographs and fond memories. They are being dismantled for their beautiful wood and torn down for safety reasons or simply because they have outlived their usefulness and the expense of upkeep isn't economically feasible for their owners. As time marches on, fewer and fewer of South Carolina's barns and farm buildings will remain.

The following pages are filled with photos of South Carolina's barns and farm buildings—most older, a few newer—as well as the people who are proud to earn their living in agriculture. These photographs have been collected from people all over the state and represent the many facets of South Carolina's rich agricultural heritage. It is our hope that those readers who are unfamiliar with this great heritage will come away with a little better understanding of life on the farm, and that readers who are familiar with such a life will feel appropriately proud and honored to be part of such a legacy.

THE LOWCOUNTRY
Allendale, Bamberg, Barnwell, Beaufort, Berkeley, Charleston, Colleton, Dorchester, Hampton and Jasper Counties

This Allendale County barn was built in 1860. Photograph courtesy of NASS.

An old pole barn stands strong on the Crider farm in Bamberg County. A new foundation and a tin roof enable the shed to remain useful and in good shape. Photograph contributed by Minnie Miller.

Located in Bamberg County, this barn was built in 1867. Photograph courtesy of NASS.

This well-kept Beaufort County barn is located on Tomotley Plantation and is surrounded by live oak trees whose branches are draped with Spanish Moss. The barn was built in 1877. Photograph courtesy of NASS.

Tomotley Plantation in Beaufort County is home to several farm structures. Photograph courtesy of NASS.

This barn is located in Beaufort County. Photograph courtesy of NASS. Collected in the 2002 Agriculture Census Old Barn Project.

This old green barn is located at Carnes Crossroads, where Highway 176 intersects Highway 17A. It was built completely by hand in 1939, without the use of electricity, using handsaws and hammers. The excellent condition of this Berkeley County landmark is a testament to quality hand-woodworking. The photograph of the interior shows a mule stall. Before an F-30 tractor was purchased, mules were used for heavy farm labor. Photographs and information contributed by Copper Welch.

This barn is located in Charleston County. Photograph courtesy of NASS. Collected in the 2002 Agriculture Census Old Barn Project.

This Charleston County barn is owned by Burnet Maybank and was built in 1840. Photograph courtesy of NASS.

This Dorchester County barn was built circa 1925. Photograph courtesy of NASS.

These three barns are all located on the farm of William Walker in Dorchester County and were built in the 1920s to house horses and cattle. Photographs courtesy of NASS.

Robert Causey DeLoach Sr. cut and sawed timber from his property to build this barn in the early 1900s. It was in use until 2000, when the property was sold. The barn, which was repainted in 2001, is located about one and a half miles south of Furman in southern Hampton County. Photograph and information contributed by Margaret M. Tuten, granddaughter of Mr. DeLoach.

This barn is located in Jasper County. Photograph courtesy of NASS. Collected in the 2002 Agriculture Census Old Barn Project.

THE PEE DEE
Chesterfield, Clarendon, Darlington, Dillon, Florence, Georgetown, Horry, Lee, Marion, Marlboro, Sumter and Williamsburg Counties

This Chesterfield County barn, known as the Griggs Hay Barn, was built in 1947 and is still in use today. Harriet White, whose grandfather built the barn and who provided the photographs and historical information, was four years old when the barn was constructed and can remember playing under the barn as a child. She also remembers that her grandfather carved toy cars for his grandsons out of blocks of wood left over from building the barn. Both photographs of the Griggs Barn show it covered in snow. The top photograph was taken in February of 1988 and the bottom photograph was taken the winter of 2001. Photographs contributed by Harriet White.

Patriotism abounds in Clarendon County. Agritourism is now part of the business on this farm. Photograph courtesy of NASS.

This barn was built in the 1930s and was renovated to its original state in 2003. It is located in Hartsville at Sugar Hill Cattle Farm, which is owned by Robert and Tim Griggs. Photograph and information contributed by Tim Griggs.

Partially covered by kudzu and surrounded by lush corn fields, this beautiful old barn is located on Highway 133 in Darlington County and was originally part of the Gandy family farm. Photograph and information contributed by Patsy Summer.

The Cross Barn stands on the rise of a hill on Highway 261 in Hemingway, which is located in Georgetown County. The lower level housed horses, mules and cattle. The upper level was used to store hay, corn and other supplies. Photograph courtesy of NASS.

THE WEATHERED OLD BARN

A stranger came by the other day with an offer that set me to thinking. He wanted to buy the old barn that sits out by the highway. I told him right off he was crazy. He was a city type, you could tell by his clothes, his car, his hands and the way he talked. He said he was driving by and saw that beautiful barn sitting out in the tall grass and wanted to know if it was for sale. I told him he had a funny idea of beauty.

Sure, it was a handsome building in its day. But then, there's been a lot of winters pass with their snow and ice and howling wind. The summer sun has beat down on that old barn until all the paint has gone and the wood has turned silver gray. Now the old building leans a good deal, looking kind of tired. Yet, that fellow called it beautiful.

That set me to thinking. I walked out to the field and just stood there, gazing at that old barn. The stranger said he planned to use the lumber to line the walls of his den in a new country home he's building down the road. He said you couldn't get paint that beautiful. Only years of standing in the weather, bearing the storms and scorching sun—only that can produce beautiful barn wood.

It came to me then. We're a lot like that, you and I. Only it's on the inside that the beauty grows with us. Sure, we turn silver gray too… and lean a bit more than we did when we were young and full of sap. But the Good Lord knows what He's doing. And as the years pass, He's busy using the hard wealth of our lives, the dry spells and the stormy seasons, to do a job of beautifying our souls that nothing else can produce. And to think how often folks holler because they want life easy!

They took the old barn down today and hauled it away to beautify the rich man's house. And I reckon someday you and I'll be hauled off to Heaven to take on whatever chores the Good Lord has for us on the Great Sky Ranch.

And I suspect we'll be more beautiful then because of the seasons we've been through here—and just maybe even add a bit of beauty to our Father's house.

Author Unknown

The barn featured in this wintry scene on Lazy Pines Road in Darlington County was built in 1945 by Chris and Ola Player. The timber used to build the barn was harvested with a cross-cut saw and it was raised exclusively with non-electric hand tools. Photograph and information contributed by Bliss S. Sports.

Located in Dillon County, Hamer Barn was built around 1900. The photograph of the barn's interior shows the wooden pegs used in the construction of the barn. Photographs and information contributed to NASS by Carl DuBose. Photographs courtesy of NASS.

This tobacco-curing barn is one of a group of five barns still standing in an oak tree grove set back from the road in Florence County. The exposed bricks show the location of the original wood-burning brick furnaces. The barn was eventually fueled by gas. Photograph and information contributed by Douglas M. Edgeworth.

This tin barn was most likely built in the 1940s. It is located on Old Quinby Road off Highway 327 in Florence County. Photograph courtesy of NASS.

The Little Red Barn is located in Georgetown County on Highway 17 between Myrtle Beach and Georgetown, and now houses a retail store. Photograph courtesy of NASS.

This barn is located in Horry County. Photograph courtesy of NASS. Collected in the 2002 Agriculture Census Old Barn Project.

Built by the Holiday family in 1928, this mule and hay barn is the largest standing barn in South Carolina. It is located at Gallivan's Ferry in Horry County and is on the National Register of Historic Places. The Holidays were the state's first tobacco growers. Photographs courtesy of NASS.

This barn is located in Horry County. Photograph courtesy of NASS. Collected in the 2002 Agriculture Census Old Barn Project.

This circa 1900s barn, located on the Johnny Johnson farm in Loris, is the type of barn used to store tobacco, hay, cotton, corn and other farm products. Photograph and information contributed by Douglas M. Edgeworth.

The shingles of this Horry County tobacco barn were blown off by Hurricane Floyd in 1999. Photograph courtesy of NASS.

This Horry County barn in Loris was built by Audie O. Gerald in the 1940s and was the first barn in the area with this kind of top. In fact, nobody in the area knew how to cut the rafters, until the pattern was revealed to Mr. Gerald one night as he slept. Upon waking, he cut a pattern for the rafters that fit perfectly and was used for many other barns in the community. Photograph and information contributed by Talbert R. Gerald, who assisted his father, Audie Gerald, in putting the roof on this barn.

A brick tobacco barn in Horry County. Photograph courtesy of NASS.

This barn was spotted along Highway 378 between Lake City and Conway. Photograph contributed by Michaele Duke.

This barn is located in Lee County. Photograph courtesy of NASS. Collected in the 2002 Agriculture Census Old Barn Project.

This Lee County barn once belonged to the Willis Woodham family and was a horse barn. It is now owned by the Rooks family. Photograph courtesy of NASS.

This Marion County barn is located on Highway 41 between 501 and 76 between Mullins and Centenary. Photograph courtesy of NASS.

Manship Homeplace in Marlboro County is home to this mule barn built in 1910. The farmstead is listed on the National Register of Historic Places. Photograph and information provided by Purvis Bedenbaugh. Photograph courtesy of NASS.

This barn (above) is located on Appin Farm, two miles west of the Marlboro County Courthouse on U.S. highways 15 and 401 West. The barn is used for storage by its owner, Richard S. Rogers, who farms the adjoining land. It has been owned by the same family since 1874. Photograph and information contributed to NASS by Catherine M. Rogers. Photograph courtesy of NASS.

Located along Highway 261 in Kingstree, this Williamsburg County barn is believed to have been built in the 1930s. Photograph and information contributed by Michaele Duke.

The Wade Barn (left), located between the towns of Dalzell and Rembert on Highway 521 in Sumter County, is around eighty years old and is most likely the smallest two-story barn in South Carolina. Photograph courtesy of NASS.

Sumter County is home to South Carolina's oldest known barn (below), located on Sans Souci Plantation. The plantation is one of very few pre–Revolutionary plantations still in existence, and is one of Sumter County's most historic sites. Sometime in the mid-eighteenth century, the Rutledge family of Charleston built their summer home in the "High Hills" and named it Sans Souci, which means "without care" or "carefree" in French. The house at Sans Souci was periodically occupied by the three Rutledge brothers. Edward Rutledge was a patriot and a statesman, and signed the Declaration of Independence. John Rutledge was the governor of South Carolina from 1782 to 1784 and chief justice of the United States Supreme Court. Hugh Rutledge was a judge and Speaker of the South Carolina General Assembly from 1782 to 1784. Sans Souci was inherited by Hugh Rutledge's daughter, Maria Huger Rutledge Waties, and later sold to the Bradley family, and then to the Mabry family. General George Mabry was a Congressional Medal of Honor recipient, and his brother, Buford Mabry, was an educator and raconteur. The Mabry brothers were raised on the property. The home was destroyed by a fire in 1934, but the ruins and the barn are still visible on the original site. Photograph courtesy of NASS.

The Benton Barrineau Barn, located in Kingstree, was built in 1954 and used to cure tobacco. The oak tree that frames the barn was one of several planted by Mr. Barrineau and his wife, Mary Agnes Coward Barrineau, in the early 1900s. Photograph and information contributed by Michaele Duke.

Captured at sunrise, this barn on McIntosh Road in Williamsburg County houses a tractor awaiting use. Photograph and information contributed by Michaele Duke.

This big red barn is located on the farm of Richard and Lisa Weaver in the Cedar Swamp Community of Kingstree in Williamsburg County. It is a cypress pole barn that has pine siding and was constructed in the 1940s. It has undergone at least two additions over the years. The roof on the barn's left side was raised to allow for the storage of large farming implements. The second addition added horse stalls to the right side of the barn. Photograph and information contributed by the Weaver family.

Bobby McCutchen's tobacco barn is located in Williamsburg County. Photograph and information contributed by Michaele Duke.

When this log barn in Williamsburg County was originally built, its owners used a wood-burning flue system to cure tobacco. Over time, it was changed to a gas system. Photograph and information provided by Douglas M. Edgeworth.

Located on Woolley Farm in the Cedar Swamp Community of Williamsburg County, this barn was built in the 1800s using pegs to support its beams. It features a drive-through corncrib, a packhouse, and housing for mules and horses. Photograph and information contributed by Douglas M. Edgeworth.

This barn is located on Mauldin Brown Farm in Kingstree. It has been converted into a horse and mule stable, and is home to Jake the mule, located in the foreground, who used to work the farm's tobacco fields. Photograph and information contributed by Douglas M. Edgeworth.

This "barn with a message" is typical of the many barns in Williamsburg County whose owners seek to communicate with passersby. It is owned by Barney and Lou Easterling and located in the Cedar Swamp area of Kingstree. Photograph and information contributed by Douglas M. Edgeworth.

Built in the 1950s, this tobacco-drying barn is located on the Billy Epps Farm in Kingstree. The ladder used by farmers to weather the tobacco until it has dried is still attached to the side of the barn. Photograph and information contributed by Douglas M. Edgeworth.

This Williamsburg County barn was owned by the late D. S. Epps and was built in the 1930s. It is located on the Old Sluter Place on I. M. Graham Road in Kingstree. Photograph and information contributed by Michaele Duke.

Owner Earle Gowdy remodeled his Hebron Crossroads barn after Hurricane Hugo struck in 1989. In 1999, it was the "Barn Again!" national winner. The annual Barn Again! Awards draw national attention to the personal efforts of farmers and ranchers who have preserved their buildings. Award-winning projects are used as models to demonstrate preservation techniques and new uses for older barns. Mr. Gowdy breeds the white, hornless goats shown in the photograph. Photograph by Michaele Duke.

THE PIEDMONT
Aiken, Calhoun, Edgefield, Fairfield, Kershaw, Lancaster, Lexington, Newberry, Orangeburg, Richland and Saluda Counties

This barn belongs to H. E. Holley and is located on Silverbluff Road in Aiken. With its scalloped eaves, this barn is reminiscent of a gingerbread house. Photograph courtesy of NASS.

This barn is located in Aiken County. Photograph courtesy of NASS. Collected in the 2002 Agriculture Census Old Barn Project.

While originally used as a horse barn, this barn in Blackstock has been used to store hay for years. Photograph and information contributed by Hope E. Brooks.

The Othniel H. Wienges brick barn was built in 1905 by a Mr. Riley. It is on Singleton Plantation, which is located on Highway 601 about three miles north of St. Matthews in Calhoun County. It was constructed with bricks made from local clay deposits. No cement was used in the barn's construction; only limestone and sand. Built to house horses and mules, it is still in use today as a horse barn. Photographs courtesy of NASS.

This barn is located in Edgefield County. Photograph courtesy of NASS. Collected in the 2002 Agriculture Census Old Barn Project.

This barn is located in Edgefield County. Photograph courtesy of NASS. Collected in the 2002 Agriculture Census Old Barn Project.

This barn is located in Fairfield County. Photograph courtesy of NASS. Collected in the 2002 Agriculture Census Old Barn Project.

This barn is located in Fairfield County. Photograph courtesy of NASS. Collected in the 2002 Agriculture Census Old Barn Project.

This barn is located in Kershaw County. Photograph courtesy of NASS. Collected in the 2002 Agriculture Census Old Barn Project.

Nothing but the roof remains of this Kershaw County barn built in 1903. Photograph courtesy of NASS.

This cultivator and barn, circa 1880, are located along old McCord Ferry Road, which was the primary transportation route between Camden and Orangeburg prior to the construction of Highway 601 South. Photograph and information contributed by Peggy Ogburn.

Located on one of the many small farms in rural Lugoff, this Kirkland family barn was built around the 1940s. The side stables housed mules and the middle portion was used to store hay. Photograph and information contributed by Beverly Kirkland.

This Lancaster County barn was built in 1900 and is located on the Wade-Beckham property currently owned by the W. W. Duke family. The Wade-Beckham house, which is listed on the National Register of Historic Places, can also be found on the property. Photograph courtesy of NASS.

This Lexington County barn is located on Old Cherokee Road. Photograph courtesy of NASS.

Built in 1938 from pine and cedar, this barn belonging to Dan Drafts is now located on the Irmo side of Lake Murray in Lexington County. It was moved from its original location near Lexington by the Drafts family in 1990 and sits in the same barnyard as the Harman barn. Photograph and information contributed by Billy Drafts.

Located on East Avenue in Leesville, this Lexington County barn sits in a large field across from the J. B. Martin Company. Photograph courtesy of J. K. York. Copyright J. K. York.

The Harman log barn was originally built near Lexington in the 1880s. In 1990, the Drafts family had it disassembled and moved to the Drafts family farm near Irmo in Lexington County. Photograph and information contributed by Billy Drafts.

Built in 1938 by the Meetze family, this barn is located in Columbia. It housed corncribs, hay lofts, stables, farm equipment and a wagon. Photograph and information contributed by Elizabeth Lindler.

This Lexington County barn, shown here just after a Southern snowfall, can be found in the town of Gilbert. Photograph courtesy of J. K. York. Copyright J. K. York.

This barn is located in Newberry County. Photograph courtesy of NASS. Collected in the 2002 Agriculture Census Old Barn Project.

The Hillcrest Dairy Barn in Orangeburg County was originally operated by South Carolina State University. It now serves as the clubhouse for the Hillcrest Golf Club. Photograph courtesy of NASS.

This new barn, located in Newberry County between Newberry and Prosperity on Highway 76, was probably built around 2004. It is used to store hay to feed the farm's horses. Photograph courtesy of NASS.

An example of what is called a pole barn, this structure's poles and shingles are made of cypress. It is located on a generations-old family farm in Orangeburg County and is thought to have been built in the 1800s. Photographs and information contributed by T. F. Riley III.

Built in the 1920s, this barn is located in Orangeburg County. Photograph courtesy of NASS.

This barn is located in Orangeburg County. Photograph courtesy of NASS. Collected in the 2002 Agriculture Census Old Barn Project.

This Richland County barn, located on the Riley family farm in Blythewood, was built in the early 1900s and was used as a dairy. Photograph and information contributed by Bryan Romig.

This barn is located in Saluda County. Photograph courtesy of NASS. Collected in the 2002 Agriculture Census Old Barn Project.

Clemson University's Sandhill Research and Education Center near Columbia in Richland County is home to this red barn. The Sandhill Farmers Market is held at the center each week from May to November. The purpose of the farmers market is to promote local agriculture by providing a place where local farmers can sell their crops, allowing the non-agricultural community to interact with agriculture and providing a venue for environmentally and agriculturally based educational activities, which are held during the market. Photograph courtesy of NASS.

The Grady Nichols barn, located in Saluda County, was built around 1937. Photograph and information contributed by Amanda Nichols.

The Robert Eleazer barn was built in 1876 and is located near Irmo in Richland County. Photograph courtesy of NASS.

This barn is located in Saluda County. Photograph courtesy of NASS. Collected in the 2002 Agriculture Census Old Barn Project.

THE UPSTATE
Abbeville, Anderson, Cherokee, Chester, Greenville, Greenwood, Laurens, McCormick, Oconee, Pickens, Spartanburg, Union and York Counties

This Abbeville County cattle and hay barn is constructed entirely of tin, and is owned by Donnie Wakefield. Photograph courtesy of NASS.

Used as a cotton storage facility, this barn is located on a National Bicentennial Farm in Abbeville County. National Bicentennial Farms are those that have remained in one family for more than two hundred years. Photograph courtesy of NASS.

Built around 1958 to 1960, this is one of South Carolina's newer barns, and can be found at Erskine College just outside of Due West. Photograph courtesy of Ed Hagan and NASS.

Captured here after an upstate snowfall, this Anderson County barn is located on the farm of the late Rufus O. Hawkins. The farm was bought by John Hawkins in 1846, and its current owner, Ted Hawkins, purchased the farm in 2001. Photograph and information contributed by Carolyn H. Grover.

Right and below: This Anderson County barn stands as an ancient monument to agriculture. Copyright J. K. York.

This barn, located in Anderson County, sits across the road from the Sandy Springs Michelin Plant, offering an architectural contrast between agriculture and industry, both of which have contributed to South Carolina's success. Photograph courtesy of NASS.

This Cherokee County barn was built in 1903. Photograph courtesy of NASS.

This barn is located in Cherokee County. Photograph courtesy of NASS. Collected in the 2002 Agriculture Census Old Barn Project.

This Cherokee County barn is located on Green River Road in Gaffney. The photograph was taken by Judy Wyles just before Christmas of 2003—note the Christmas star affixed to the roof. Photograph courtesy of NASS. Collected in the 2002 Agriculture Census Old Barn Project.

This circa 1890 barn is located on Beaver Dam Road in Gaffney and features a hand-hewn log interior and additions dating to the 1950s. Photograph by Judy Wyles and courtesy of NASS. Collected in the 2002 Agriculture Census Old Barn Project.

This barn is located in Chester County. Photograph courtesy of NASS. Collected in the 2002 Agriculture Census Old Barn Project.

This barn was built in 1924 on Cotton Hills Farm in Lowrys, located in Chester County. The farm itself has operated continuously since 1882 when the original one-hundred-acre homeplace was given to Theodosia Abell Wilson as a wedding present. Current owners Jeff and Carol Wilson and their children are the fourth generation to work the land, now producing many acres of cotton, corn, wheat, hay, pumpkins, and timber. The family sells a large variety of merchandise, including cotton crafts, honey, jellies, relishes, butter, salsa, syrup and their own stone-ground grits and meal. The Wilson family also supports agritourism in South Carolina by offering living classroom and family farm tours, which include wagon rides, picnics, a petting zoo, camping and hiking trips, a turn-of-the-century tractor-engine-operated grist mill, a corn maze, and educational sessions. Photograph courtesy of NASS.

This large mule barn in Chester County was built in 1915. It is owned by Margaret Housman, who now houses cattle in the barn. Photograph courtesy of NASS.

This barn is located in Greenville County. Photograph courtesy of NASS. Collected in the 2002 Agriculture Census Old Barn Project.

This barn is located in Greenville County. Photograph courtesy of NASS. Collected in the 2002 Agriculture Census Old Barn Project.

This dairy barn is located on the campus of Bob Jones University in Greenville County. Photograph courtesy of NASS.

The Blue Ridge Mountains provide a scenic backdrop to this upstate barn located in Greenville County. Photograph courtesy of NASS.

As a result of urban sprawl, this Greenville County barn no longer stands. Photograph and information contributed by Brian Kelley.

This Greenville County barn is located at the Roper Mountain Science Center's Living Farm. Photograph by Clemson University County Extension Agent Danny Howard.

This barn is located in the state's Upcountry region and is still in use today. Photograph and information contributed by Melissa Stover.

These barns were built in the 1930s or 1940s as part of a Hereford cattle farm in Moonville. Acquired in 1978 by Eddie and Debbie Candler, the old barns have been replaced by a newer and larger horse barn. The combination of the setting sun and the glistening snow-covered barns made for this beautiful photograph taken in 1982.

This black and white photo of the Candler family barns, located in Moonville, offers a more close-up view of the structures. Photograph courtesy of NASS.

Every Christmas for nearly forty years, the Edwards family has hung a green wreath on their barn in Taylors. The barn has long been a favorite place for family gatherings, get-togethers and bonfires. Photograph and information contributed by Roger Edwards Dempsey.

This barn is located in Greenwood County. Photograph courtesy of NASS. Collected in the 2002 Agriculture Census Old Barn Project.

The sun was just rising as the camera captured this Greenwood County barn. The barn is part of the Epworth Community and hosts the community's camp meetings. Photograph courtesy of NASS.

This barn is located in Greenwood County. Photograph courtesy of NASS. Collected in the 2002 Agriculture Census Old Barn Project.

Located in Laurens County, this cattle and hay barn was rebuilt about twenty years ago after a storm destroyed the original structure. Photograph courtesy of NASS.

The Works Progress Administration (WPA), the largest and most important of the New Deal cultural programs, was a massive employment relief program launched in the spring of 1935. The WPA's purpose was to put unemployed Americans back to work in jobs that would serve the public good and conserve the skills and the self-esteem of the workers. This dairy barn was built in 1931 by WPA workers and was part of the John De La Howe School for orphans. The school's students milked cows as part of a work-school program. While the barn ceased to house dairy cows in 1980, it is still in use. Its lower level is now a retail shop and its upper level is a venue for community events. One interesting feature of the barn is an underground tunnel that was used to move cattle to and from the pasture across the road. Photograph courtesy of NASS.

This barn is located in McCormick County. Photograph courtesy of NASS. Collected in the 2002 Agriculture Census Old Barn Project.

McCormick County residents show their Clemson University pride by painting large orange tiger paws on their barns. The photograph of the red barn with the tiger paw over the door was provided by NASS.

The other barn, which features two tiger paws, is owned by Douglass K. Britt and is located northwest of McCormick on Highway 28. It was built in 1950 by Samuel Leslie Britt, the father of the current owner, and was used to store hay for his cattle. Mr. Samuel Britt cut the timber himself from sweetgum, sycamore and pine trees in order to construct the two-story barn. He was a 1911 graduate of Clemson University, where he majored in animal husbandry and, along with two of his brothers, played football for the Clemson Tigers. Photograph courtesy of NASS.

This barn is located in Oconee County. Photograph courtesy of NASS. Collected in the 2002 Agriculture Census Old Barn Project.

The Tokeena barn in Seneca has been in the McPhail family for over a century. The photo at right shows the family of J. A. and Mary Stevenson McPhail in front of the original structure in 1902. The photo above shows the barn as it appears today, along with many members of the current McPhail family. The entire farm complex, which is 190 acres in size and includes tenant houses, a corncrib and other buildings in addition to the barn, is listed on the National Register of Historic Places. The photograph at right and information contributed by Neil and Gwen McPhail. The photograph above by Brian Roberts.

This Pickens County barn, surrounded by splendid fall colors, is owned by Buck Hinkle and is located on Eastatoe Community Road in the upper part of Eastatoe Valley. Photograph by Bob Spalding.

This barn is located in Oconee County. Photograph courtesy of NASS. Collected in the 2002 Agriculture Census Old Barn Project.

Located in Easley, this Pickens County barn is one of South Carolina's newer barns. It was built around 1985 by James P. Tumlin, who bought the land it sits on some fifty years ago from his father. At the time the barn was built, Mr. James Tumlin was raising Black Angus cows and used the barn to store hay for his cattle. After retiring from the cattle business, Mr. Tumlin turned the barn into rental space. It is currently the photography studio of Lorrie Morey, owner of Morey Photography, who took this photograph and provided the historical information about the barn.

This Spartanburg County hay and mule barn was built well before 1920, probably between 1910 and 1915. The parents of Marie Johns, who works in the South Carolina Field Office of the USDA's National Agricultural Statistics Service, own the farm on which the barn is located.

This Foster Farms barn is a National Bicentennial Barn located in Spartanburg County's town of Inman. National Bicentennial Farms are those that have remained in one family for more than two hundred years. Photograph courtesy of NASS.

This Spartanburg County barn was built circa 1875. Photograph courtesy of NASS.

This barn and its silo are located in Inman. Photograph courtesy of NASS.

Built in 1852, this Meador Plantation barn shown in these three photographs was restored by Don West Painting and its owners, Wayne and Sharyn Wallace, and is shown before, during and after restoration. Due to its secluded location, the barn survived General Sherman's rampage through Sumter National Park during the Civil War. Photograph and information contributed by Don West Painting.

Located in Union County on the Meador Plantation, this barn is owned by Wayne and Sharyn Wallace. It was built in 1852 and housed sheep, cattle and Confederate soldiers returning home from the Civil War. At the time of publication, the barn was being restored by its owners and Don West Painting. Photograph and information contributed by Don West Painting.

This barn is located in Union County. Photograph courtesy of NASS. Collected in the 2002 Agriculture Census Old Barn Project.

Built in 1961, this barn is part of the Flying King Ranch in York County. Photograph courtesy of NASS.

Located at a crossroads in Santuc, this Union County barn was built in the early 1900s to house animals and store hay. Photograph and information contributed by Don West Painting.

This eight-sided octagonal cattle barn has eight doors and was built around 1939 or 1940 by Matthew Lewis Elder, the great uncle of current owner Lewis "Sonny" Elder Moore Jr. It is located on Chester Highway in McConnells, a town in York County. While it was originally a dairy barn, it is now used to store hay and feed. Its unique shape and picturesque facade make it a favorite subject for local painters, as well as passing motorists who have their cameras with them. Photograph courtesy of NASS and information provided by Sonny Moore.

THE BARNS OF CLEMSON UNIVERSITY

The 1902 Experiment Station Barn, the barn closest to Clemson University's central campus, is located on Cherry Road. The barn has taken on the popular name of "The Sheep Barn," although it was only used temporarily for sheep from the late 1930s to the early 1940s. The brick and wood structure currently serves as a support location for the University's facilities and maintenance operations. When the barn was originally constructed by the Experiment Station, it was used to study specific breeds of cattle. Photograph by Brian Roberts.

Pictured here at moonrise, Clemson University's old dairy barn complex is one of the most recognizable symbols of the University's land grant heritage. Its prominent location at the corner of Perimeter and Old Stone Church roads ensures that hundreds of thousands of students, employees and visitors view the dairy complex each year. The complex was originally developed in 1911 and now also includes buildings constructed in 1930 (wood) and 1935 (brick). It was originally built to house the University's dairy herd, which provided milk for campus dining services, as well as for the making of Clemson's famous blue cheese and ice cream in later years. Buildings in the dairy complex are now used as a support facility for the Walker Golf Course and for turf-grass research. Photograph by Brian Roberts.

The architecturally unique J. C. Stribling barn at "Sleepy Hollow" is located almost mid-way between Clemson University's campus and Farmer's Hall on the Town Square in Pendleton, where in the late 1800s Thomas Green Clemson first spoke of establishing Clemson A&M College. The entire property, including the beautiful brick barn, was restored in the 2000s and is now a popular bed and breakfast and special event venue.

The barn was built in 1900 by Jesse Cornelius Stribling (1844–1927) and is architecturally significant as an impressive and atypical example of barn design and construction from the turn of the twentieth century. Built into the side of a hill to allow ground-level access to all stories, this style of barn is commonly known as a "bank barn." This form is usually found in New England and the Midwest, but is relatively rare in the Southeast. Additionally, its construction of brick rather than weatherboard siding is even more unusual in the region and in South Carolina. The barn's high roofline and front entrance gable give the barn a late-Victorian-period appearance. The jerkinhead-shaped, V-crimp metal-clad roof, with a steeply pitched intersecting gable over the main entry, is supported by eight square wood piers and corresponding timber trusses. The 140,000 native red bricks used in its construction were hand-made on site and vary in color from terra cotta to dark umber. The late Victorian appearance is enhanced by decorative latticed brickwork found around the windows and in the main entrance gable. The Stribling barn was listed in the National Register on October 22, 2001. (Architectural information reprinted with permission from the South Carolina Department of Archives and History, www.nationalregister.sc.gov/pickens/S10817739020/index.htm.) Photograph by Brian Roberts.

The Woodburn Plantation brick barn (above) and the Block and Bridle Club barn are located just off Highway 76 across from Tri-County Technical College in Pendleton, a historic town in Anderson County. The barns are part of the Woodburn Plantation property, which was originally established in 1830 by Charles Cotesworth Pinckney of Charleston, who served as lieutenant governor of South Carolina from 1832 to 1834 and was a member of the South Carolina family that included two signers of the United States Constitution. The property was expanded over the years to include the original house and the brick barn. The club barn, which is a clapboard structure, was constructed more recently.

The property has had more than eleven caretakers in its history. Clemson University served as steward of the property from 1954 until 1966, when the federal government's Resettlement Administration/Land Policy Section of the Agricultural Adjustment Administration placed the property under long-term lease to Clemson College. Since then, the barns and pastures have been utilized by the agricultural entities of the University, while the Pendleton Historic Foundation owns the property. The four-story plantation house is listed on the National Register of Historic Places. Clemson University and the College of Agriculture, Forestry and Life Sciences student clubs utilize the barns for various events, research and instruction. The photograph of the brick barn is courtesy of NASS. The photograph of the club barn was taken by Brian Roberts.

The T. Ed Garrison Livestock Arena, fondly referred to as "The Red Hoof Inn" by students, is located near Highway 76 on Clemson University's research and farm properties. It is recognized as one of the premier multi-purpose livestock facilities in the Southeast. The facility includes two acres of under-roof show arena with three thousand seats, four barns with 440 stalls, vending space and expanded facilities for special events. Events held at the Garrison Arena draw thousands of visitors to Clemson and South Carolina, boost tourism significantly and contribute to economic development in the Upstate and throughout the entire state. Photograph by Brian Roberts.

WORKING BUILDINGS, EQUIPMENT AND LIFE ON THE FARM

This log smokehouse is more than one hundred years old and was recently restored for preservation. Photograph and information contributed by Ben Teal of Patrick, South Carolina.

The Horton family operated Horton's Mill, located on Highway 151 just north of McBee, for at least seventy-five years. Its sign advertises "Fresh Meal Grits Ground Daily." The current status is not known. Photographs and information contributed by Walter K. Lewis Jr.

This old outhouse is located on the property owned by the Brooks family in Blackstock. Hope E. Brooks, who contributed the photograph, said her family considered this to be the deluxe model because it had two seats, rather than just one.

Vines have almost completely covered this old windmill. The windmill was originally located on the farm of Nellie Herring between Mont Clair and Society Hill, but it can now be found on Mineral Springs Road off Highway 52 between Dovesville and Darlington. Photograph and information contributed by Patsy Summer.

Clemson graduate Whitney C. Weatherly calls this photograph "The Windsical Forces of Nature," because it evokes images of the various forces of nature experienced in Sumter: wind, freezing rain, centrifugal force, time, below-freezing temperatures and gravity.

This old water spigot provided hand-pumped water from a well in Lake City. Photograph contributed by Karen C. Hall.

This photograph (above) is entitled "Retired Disc." Taken by Karen Creel, it pictures an old disc that was used by her grandfather to work his fields on Fore Farm, which is located in Fork, a town in Dillon County.

This photograph by Karen C. Hall shows old tobacco-planting equipment on the farm of Al Williamson, a Lake City tobacco farmer.

New corn grows in front of this old single-family house (above). Located on Running Brook Road in Darlington County, it was the home of Voight Q. Gandy and his family. Patsy Summer, who contributed the photograph and information, says the sound of rain on a tin roof, like the one seen in this photograph, was a wonderful sound.

This storage shed, which features a unique door, sits in the side yard of Mary Carrigan's property in Society Hill. Photograph contributed by Patsy Summer.

When the home of the Robert Baker family burned in 1908, they moved into this packhouse (above), adding windows at that time to make it into a house. It still stands on the Baker family's West Cades farm in Williamsburg County. Photograph and information provided by Douglas M. Edgeworth.

Allie Snell was a farmer and rural mail carrier for the post office in Parler, a small town located in Orangeburg County. This photograph, taken in the early 1900s, shows Allie and an unidentified mailman bidding goodbye to Allie's wife Julia before setting out to deliver the day's mail. Photograph and information provided by the Elloree Heritage Museum.

John F. Brandon of Union visits the farm upon which he grew up. Known as "The Homeplace," the Union County farm was already beginning to crumble in 1900. Photograph and information provided by M. Blake Berry.

An annual production sale took place at Tri S Ranch in Calhoun Falls every year from 1962 to 1982. More than a thousand people attended each sale, and, on average, two hundred to four hundred head of cattle were sold to buyers from some ten states. Photograph and information provided by Rufus C. Sherard.

Attendees of the 1954 or 1955 American Dairy Association Convention are pictured here from left to right: W. L. Abernathy, Sam McGregor, Harriet and Ozzie Nelson of The Adventures of Ozzie and Harriet *fame, J. P. Rogers and Ed Garrison. Photograph provided by Sam McGregor.*

The four eldest children of W. H. McPhail take a break from helping on the McPhail Angus farm, located on Pine Grove Road in Seneca, to play in the creek below an old tenant house behind the barn. Photograph and information provided by Neil McPhail.

Grace Moore takes a break from riding and stands in the shade with her Paso Fino named Bolero. Grace and her grandmother, Joan Pennington, ride often on the peaceful dirt roads and farmlands of Saluda. Photograph provided by Leigh Moore.

Tim Griggs, owner of Sugar Hills Farm in Hartsville, and his Shorthaired Pointer named Dixie, in a cotton field. Photograph provided by Tim Griggs.

Clemson graduate Laurie Ulmer and his six-year-old son, Rivers, look down from the loft of the old barn on the Ulmer Farm in Elloree. Photograph provided by Marykay Martin.

Located on Highway 377 in Williamsburg County, the John Gamble home was built in 1927 by James Oliver and Jennie Bostick Gamble from local timber milled at their sawmill in Heineman. The live oak tree is one of seven registered with the Louisiana Live Oak Society. It has been named the "Wedding Oak," and Sarah Sylvan Gamble, granddaughter of James O. Gamble, was married under it on April 27, 1996. Photograph by Michaele Duke.

The hand towel says it all. Photograph provided by David Jameson of Aiken.

This 1962 photograph shows (from left to right) siblings Kirby, James, Kathy and Bobby Johnson, as they survey the late-season cotton crop at their daddy's gin. Living next door to the gin, they were never too far from cotton production. Photograph provided by Miriam Johnson.

Becky Wood is pictured here with a child's saddle that is forty years old, which she beautifully restored for Sheila Someral of Hickory Tavern. Becky and her husband, Greg, own Britten-Wood Highlanders Farm, located in Gray Court.

A combine harvester makes its way through downtown Bishopville, an unintentional but appropriate tribute to the contribution small towns and agriculture make to society. The combine harvester, often referred to simply as a combine, combines the tasks of harvesting, threshing and cleaning grain crops such as wheat, oats, rye, barley, corn, soybeans and flax. Photograph by Charlie Ogg.

Joseph Rickenbacker sells collards, mustard greens and turnips on the main drag in Bamberg. Says Rickenbacker, "They're as sweet as me!" Photograph by Minnie Miller.

Greg and Becky Wood, owners of Britten-Wood Highlanders Farm in Gray Court, raise beautiful highlander cattle. They take joy in sharing the beautiful creatures with others and routinely do school and church group demonstrations. Pictured here wearing homemade cowboy boots are Becky and Greg with Sparky, who is dressed in his finest for the annual Christmas photo.

Pictured here is a tin-sided barbecue pit used by Carl Kinlaw to roast pigs for family holidays and special occasions too numerous to count. It was not uncommon for this pit to cook fourteen pigs at a time.

BARBECUE—THE TASTE, FELLOWSHIP AND FUN OF SOUTH CAROLINA

By Saddler Taylor

Barbecue in South Carolina is a story of struggle, interdependence, joy and improvisation. It's about people, shared traditions and a sense of place. To understand barbecue history in the Palmetto State is to acknowledge the contributions of multiple traditions: African, Native American and European. Once separate streams, these traditions flowed together early in the state's history to form the mighty river that is South Carolina slow-cooked pork. The more time a person spends around piles of felled hardwood, smoke-stained cook sheds and cast iron hash pots, the clearer one thing becomes: barbecue is not a tradition to be romanticized. Enjoyed now as comfort food, barbecue has roots in a culture of improvisation and survival. For hundreds of years, slow-cooked whole hog was a way for people to prepare an available staple. Well into the twentieth century, rural farmers cooked hogs for supplemental income and communities frequently pooled resources to fire up a pot of hogshead or beef hash.

Early colonists found the hog perfectly suited for conditions in the South. Low maintenance and manageable in size, hogs could be let loose to fend for themselves in the thick forests of Virginia and the Carolinas. In the case of the small farmer, the butchering and cooking of a hog was not only a necessary part of life; it provided family and friends with an important social occasion. This was a community event. Neighbors assisted with the cooking, musicians turned out fiddle tunes, children stood "at the elbows" of the older folks stirring the hash pot. Stories were told around the barbecue pit, back porch and kitchen table. Problems were shared, gossip told. This was a time of release from the vagaries of working the rock-strewn fields of the Piedmont, the sandy soil of the Pee Dee or the rice fields in the Santee Delta. Barbecue was about the dirty, sweaty work of digging a pit in the backyard and eviscerating hogs. But it was also about the joys shared by family and friends—life's celebrations and struggles. Local foodways were inseparable from the seasonal nature of agrarian life.

Traditional South Carolina barbecue is rooted in family and community culture. Long before formal barbecue restaurants were established, folks traveled county roads selling barbecue from the trunk of the family car or the bed of the pickup truck. Those who developed reputations as skilled pit masters were soon in demand and were called on by churches, civic groups and other community organizations to fire up the pit for an annual fundraiser or social event. These early barbecue cooks mastered the catering business long before catering became a standardized industry.

The barbecue restaurant we know today was born out of this itinerant pit master tradition and family "shade tree" cooking. Unlike the collective petri dish of mass-produced food, South Carolina's local barbecue joints maintain a firm grip on their agricultural heritage. While many have phased out such traditional delicacies as souse, liver pudding, and hogshead hash, they have a clear vision of their past and their roots. Symbolism runs high—PawPaw's cast iron kettle, Dad's heralded sauce recipe, Auntie's special coleslaw. In most cases, the restaurant is less about food and more about the people behind the recipes, the socially rich process of cooking and the equally important act of consumption.

A deliciously flavored barbecued pork shoulder is ready for pullin' at Ridgeway, South Carolina's Pig on the Ridge BBQ Cook-off.

During South Carolina's turbulent history, enslaved Africans, sharecroppers, marginalized Native Americans and Upstate mill workers cultivated dynamic food traditions. These culture groups did not exist in a vacuum. Blacks, whites and Native Americans prepared and consumed foods that were readily available, while constantly reinventing their respective cuisine through the influences of surrounding cultural traditions. Regional South Carolina barbecue was born largely through Native American cooking methods, African seasoning and the swine of European settlers.

No matter the particular sauce or ingredients—chicken bog, hash, puddin' pot, whole hog barbecue—all of the traditions maintain regional differences that reflect the diversity of the environment and the people doing the cooking. Barbecue continues to be about sustaining a sense of community. But why such variety? Like a folk artist maintains a sense of individuality while perfecting certain skills under the tutelage of family, friends or community members, barbecue chefs and hash masters add their own signature to the recipes of past generations.

Surrounded by nostalgia, barbecue can serve as a way to honor ancestors who labored during a much different time. The ears, hearts and tongue of hogshead hash are no longer savored because survival depends on using every bit of the hog. Today hash masters can afford to make hash out of the "finer" cuts: shoulder, Boston butts and hams. Yet, if you look in the right places, you can still find a fine batch of hogshead

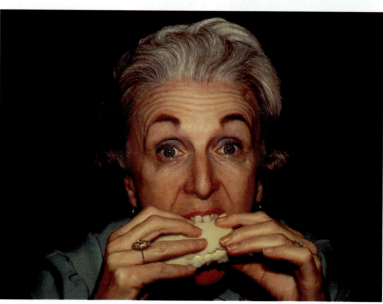

Miss Ernestine Player of Columbia enjoys pulled-pork barbecue at its simplest—and some would say best—on white bread with mayonnaise. Mmm mmm good!

or liver hash roiling in a pot. Symbolism and tradition are powerful social binders that reaffirm community identity. These deeply held traditions are felt by fewer people today. The cultural demographic is changing. Prior to the 1960s, getting some barbecue meant one of two things: you either did the cooking yourself or you knew those folks in the community whose culinary reputation preceded them. We have it easy now. On any given day, good barbecue can be found on a buffet line somewhere in the state. Fortunately, there are still those who value the toil and struggle of the early barbecue pioneers and their vigilance allows us to enjoy a heaping plate of South Carolina history.

Saddler Taylor is chief curator of Folklife and Research for McKissick Museum at the University of South Carolina. Originally published as an article in the Fall 2006 edition of Edible Lowcountry *magazine, this text is reprinted in part and with minor editorial changes with the permission of the author and publisher.*

Venison cube steaks are dipped in batter before being fried to perfection at the annual Wild Game Banquet in Bamberg. Photograph by Minnie Miller.

Two hungry hunters take a break from the hunt to slurp oysters at the annual Wild Game Banquet in Bamberg County. Photograph by Minnie Miller.

SOUTH CAROLINA'S FOUR TYPES OF BARBECUE SAUCE

By Lake E. High Jr., President, South Carolina Barbeque Association

There are generally considered to be four types of barbecue in America. By and large, they are broken down by the type of basting sauce—rubbed on the meat as it is cooking—and the type of finishing sauce—poured over the barbecue when it is being served and eaten. These four types of barbecue, in order of historical emergence, are Vinegar and Pepper, Mustard, Light Tomato, and Heavy Tomato. And while culinary opinions differ about methods of preparation, such as whether a dry rub or a wet rub is best, all of the many sauces used in America generally fall into one of these four basic groups.

North and South Carolina share three of the four types of barbecue sauce found in America. But only South Carolina is home to all four.

The "original" barbecue sauce, which dates back hundreds—yes, hundreds—of years, is Vinegar and Pepper, the oldest and simplest of the four sauces. It is found on the coastal plains of both North and South Carolina and to a lesser degree in Virginia and Georgia. The Scottish families who settled primarily in present-day Williamsburg County in South Carolina's lowcountry are the state's most famous preparers of Vinegar and Pepper barbecue. The Brown family is one of South Carolina's most prominent Scottish barbecue families. Other recognized names include McKenzie, Scott and McCabe, all of whom have remained true to their heritage in their preparation of barbecue.

The second of the four sauces, in order of historic emergence, is the one that is distinct to South Carolina and the one that people most often think of as South Carolina-style: Mustard Sauce. This sauce is the product of the large German heritage found in South Carolina.

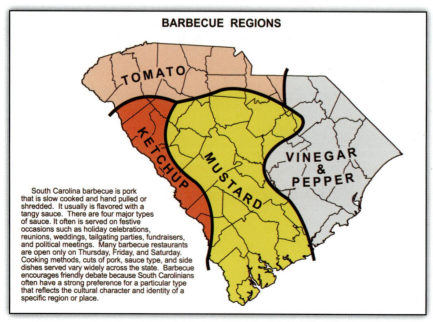

Source: Kovacik and Winberry, *South Carolina: A Geography*, 1987, p. 209.

Starting in the 1730s and continuing into the 1750s, the British colony of South Carolina encouraged, recruited and even paid the ocean passage for thousands of German families to settle in South Carolina. They were a hardworking, sturdy and resourceful people, given to an intensive family-farm type of agriculture, as opposed to the plantation system favored by the English settlers.

These German families were given land grants up the Santee, Congaree, Broad and Saluda rivers over a more than twenty-year immigration period. These rivers all flow into each other and flow from the upcountry to the lowcountry of the state. The first settlements were located in what is today Dorchester County. Later arrivals settled further up the rivers in the present-day counties of Orangeburg, Lexington, Newberry and the northwestern part of Richland County. In addition to their European farming style and the Lutheran Church, the settlers introduced the common use of mustard to South Carolina.

The evidence of the German settlers' influence on South Carolina's mustard barbecue sauce is still in evidence today, some 250 years later, in the names of the state's families who sell mustard-based sauces and mustard-based barbecue to the public. The Bessinger family name is legendary in South Carolina's mustard-based barbecue business. Other well-known German names in the business include Shealy, Hite, Sweatman, Sikes, Price, Lever, Meyer, Kiser and Zeigler. Dooley's Barbecue in Lexington County bears the name of a family with its roots in Germany, not Ireland as many assume. Dooley is derived from the German surname Dula (pronounced Doole), as in the infamous Thomas Dula who became "Tom Dooley" in The Kingston Trio's 1960s song, "Hang Down Your Head, Tom Dooley."

Light Tomato Sauce was the third type of sauce to emerge in South Carolina. This sauce is—or was—little more than the original Vinegar and Pepper Sauce with tomato ketchup added. When tomato ketchup became readily available around 1900, it was simple to add a bit of that spicy condiment to the tried and true Vinegar and Pepper Sauce, bringing a little sweetness and other spices into the mix. This style of sauce is most famous in North Carolina's Piedmont region, where Lexington, North Carolina, the acknowledged barbecue center of the state, is located. It is also popular in the upper middle part of South Carolina and in South Carolina's Pee Dee region, the upper coastal plain area of the state.

The fourth and final sauce to surface was Heavy Tomato Sauce. This sauce has evolved over time, and has only recently, in the last sixty or so years, come to be considered a major type of barbecue sauce. It has spread rapidly over the majority of the nation due to modern transportation, modern marketing, and the insatiable sweet tooth of modern Americans.

Heavy Tomato Sauce is most often seen in the types of sauces popularized by the food industry and, as a result, has found its way onto the shelves of just about every grocery store and supermarket in the country. Heavy Tomato Sauce is what most Americans (but not Carolinians) think of when they think of barbecue sauce.

PEPPER & VINEGAR SAUCE
Contributed by David and Zetty Bell

This favorite recipe for Carolina Vinegar and Pepper Sauce is a little different than most.

- 1   gallon of white vinegar
- 8   ounces of crushed red pepper
- 4   tablespoons of dark brown sugar
- 4   tablespoons of paprika
- 1   6-ounce bottle of Texas Pete hot sauce
- 1   cup of pickling salt

If more spiciness is desired, add 4 tablespoons ground cayenne pepper.

Mix all ingredients in a large container and allow mixture to age until the pepper seeds sink to the bottom of the container. To serve, shake the large container of sauce well and then pour sauce into containers about 1 pint in size.

Add 2 tablespoons of melted butter or put butter into sauce and heat slowly. The result will be a slightly hot and wonderfully smooth sauce. Buttered sauce should be refrigerated.

Brian Bowen (left), Bobby Bowen (middle) and Hart Coker Jr. discuss the progress of the pig they are roasting at a family gathering, while Bonnie Bowen and Shannon Coker (far right) look on.

PEE DEE RED SAUCE (LIGHT TOMATO)

- 1   cup of white vinegar (or apple cider vinegar if preferred)
- 1   cup of sugar (Karo syrup can be used)
- 1 1/2   cups of good ketchup (Heinz is good)
- 2 to 3   teaspoons of black pepper (start with 2 and add a third teaspoon if a stronger black pepper taste is desired)
- 2   teaspoons of hot sauce (Trappies or Texas Pete are both good) or use 2 teaspoons of red pepper flakes

This is a much better sauce than the thick tomato-based sauces sold in stores. Not only is it a good finishing sauce, but it can be used as a topping for slaw. When this recipe is used for a basting sauce, white vinegar works well; when used as a topping for slaw, apple cider vinegar is best.

A red sauce is really more of a "finishing" sauce applied to the barbecue an hour or so before it is taken off the fire. Red sauces are generally not used as "basting" sauces; sauces used to baste the meat for the many hours that barbecue has to be cooked to be properly called "barbecue." Red sauces have too much sugar in them to work really well as basting sauces.

Hart Coker Sr. (right) of Clemson stands with his son, Hart Coker Jr., in front of the oil-drum roaster he designed himself and then built from scratch. To celebrate Father's Day in 2009, the Coker family spent the day together outside in Central while Hart Jr. slow-roasted a pig on the cooker his dad made for him.

GOLDEN MUSTARD BARBECUE SAUCE

Contributed by Walter Brooker of Denmark, South Carolina, senior judge for the South Carolina Barbeque Association and pit master of Team Squeal Appeal

1	cup of white vinegar
1/2	cup of prepared yellow mustard
1/4	cup of Dijon mustard
1	medium onion, minced
1/3	cup of water
1/4	cup of tomato paste
1	tablespoon of paprika
2	tablespoons of brown sugar
7	cloves of garlic, minced
2	teaspoons of celery salt
1/2	teaspoon of cayenne
1/2	teaspoon of freshly ground black pepper

Place all of the ingredients into a non-reactive heavy-bottomed saucepan. Place the pan over medium high heat and bring the mixture to a simmer. Reduce heat to low and cook for 25 minutes until the mixture thickens and the onions are tender. Serve warm or cold. This sauce will keep for 2 weeks covered in the refrigerator.

The Munnerlyn family gets together every Christmas. Even though half the family members are University of South Carolina fans and the other half are Clemson fans, they have a great time barbecuing, playing football in the yard and hunting.

MUSTARD BBQ SAUCE

Contributed by Lake E. High Jr., president of the South Carolina Barbeque Association

1	cup of Kraft mustard
2/3	cup of Karo syrup (dark if you have it)
2/3	cup of ketchup
1/3	cup of white vinegar
1	teaspoon of dill weed
1	teaspoon of ground allspice
1	teaspoon of hot pepper sauce
1/2	teaspoon of black pepper
3	teaspoons of liquid smoke
1/2	tablespoon of sorghum
1/3	tablespoon of Lea & Perrin Worcestershire sauce

Mix all ingredients together. Double or triple this recipe and keep it on hand in the refrigerator for a few weeks.

A team of barbecue-cooking experts smile for the camera during Ridgeway's annual Pig on the Ridge Cook-off.

JT'S BBQ FOOT HILLS BBQ SAUCE
Contributed by Tim Handy, pit master of JT's BBQ Competition cooking team

8	cups of Hunt's ketchup
2 1/2	cups of White House cider vinegar
1 1/2	cups of Worcestershire sauce
1 1/2	cups of water
3	tablespoons of Colgin's liquid smoke
2	cups of white sugar
4	cups of dark brown sugar
5	tablespoons of yellow mustard
5	tablespoons of salt
1	tablespoon of black pepper
3	tablespoons of chili powder
3	teaspoons of paprika
1/3	cup of cooking oil

Combine all ingredients in a heavy-duty aluminum pot. Slowly bring to a simmer for 20 minutes. Allow the sauce to cool before serving.

It is actually not unusual for folks to cook barbecue in the trunk of their car. Pictured here are cooks in front of their Monte Carlo barbecue pit during the annual Q-Cup Cook-off.

Hog Wild cooking team members proudly show off their final product at one of South Carolina's many barbecue contests.

GLORIFIED VIDALIA ONIONS

5 to 6	medium sweet Vidalia onions
1/2	cup of apple cider vinegar
1	cup of sugar
2	cups of water
1/2	cup of mayonnaise (or more to your taste)
1	teaspoon of celery seed

Finely chop (for spread or condiment) or thinly slice (for slaw or cracker topping) onions. In a large airtight container, mix together vinegar, sugar and water. Stir until sugar is completely dissolved. Submerse onions in solution, ensuring all onions are covered. Soak onions in the water, sugar and vinegar for 4 hours or overnight, stirring or shaking the solution to shift mixture. Drain well. Pat onions dry (use paper towels to squeeze out excess brine).

Mix onions with mayonnaise and celery seed. Serve with buttery crackers, toasted breads, on meats or as a "slaw like" side.

Note: The finer you can chop the onions, the better for spread or dip.

The Salt and Pepper cooking team members display the result of their hard work during the annual Q-Cup Cook-off.

JT'S BBQ BREAKFAST PIE
Contributed by Tim Handy, Pit Master of JT's BBQ Competition cooking team

2   deep-dish frozen pie shells
1   roll of spicy whole hog bulk sausage
1   large Vidalia onion
1   large green bell pepper
1   dozen large farm eggs
2   packs of shredded sharp cheddar cheese (4 cups)
2   tablespoons of bacon grease

Sautee the onion and bell pepper in the bacon grease. Add the whole hog bulk sausage and brown. Drain the sausage mixture and divide it between the two pie shells. Beat six eggs for each pie and pour over sausage mixture. Top the pies with cheese and bake at 350 degrees for 30 to 45 minutes. Remove from the oven and allow to rest for 15 minutes before slicing.

The South Carolina Barbeque Association is dedicated to training the world's best barbeque judges. Pictured here are three judges who have been certified by the organization.

The Fourth of July is the perfect occasion for an outdoor barbecue. Keith Edgeworth hosted family and friends at his home in Johnston to celebrate the freedom we all enjoy in America.

SWEET PEPPER RELISH
Contributed by Elizabeth Meaders

12   red bell peppers
12   green bell peppers
12   large onions

Grind finely, all together, peppers and onions. Pour boiling water over ground vegetables and let stand for five minutes. Drain.

Add:
2   cups of sugar
3   cups of vinegar (either white or apple cider—apple cider is usually thought to have a better flavor)

In a non-aluminum pan,* boil mixture at a rolling boil for five minutes. Place in sterilized jars** and seal.

*Never cook pickle-type mixtures in aluminum pans; they will turn the color of both pan and pickles.

**Jars, lids and rings can be washed in the dishwasher's hottest cycle to sterilize. If boiling jars to sterilize, do not put the rings in boiling water or they'll expand too much—put the rings in water that is hot, but not boiling.

A hunting excursion is one of the oldest and fondest forms of fellowship. Pictured here after a full day of hunting quail are (standing from left to right) Irvin Plowden Jr., Dan Plowden, Blain Player, Irvin Plowden Sr. and (kneeling) Kirby Player.

ERIE HIGH'S BEANS AND SPROUTS
Contributed by Lake E. High Jr.

3 to 4	slices of bacon
1	medium onion, chopped
1/2	large bell pepper, chopped
1/4	cup of ketchup
1	large can of Pork 'n Beans (Van Camp's or Bush's Original are good. Don't use those that have been sugared; there is enough sugar in the ketchup.)

Cook the bacon slices until crisp, place on paper to drain and cool, then crumble. Chop the onion and pepper and sauté in remaining bacon grease.

Add the pork and beans and the ketchup to the pan and stir. Add the crumbled bacon pieces. Allow mixture to simmer for about an hour, until it thickens.

This recipe can easily be multiplied—it's always just as good. As Daddy used to say, "Not many people refuse 'um."

Regardless of what team a person pulls for, tailgating before (and during… and after…) a football game brings family and friends from near and far together in a special kind of way. The excitement of game day combined with the feeling of camaraderie evokes a sense of oneness, anticipation, belonging and exhilaration all at the same time.

Sisters Sandra Jameson of Aiken and Jackie Crosby of Charleston inherited their family's 150-year-old farmhouse. The sisters updated it with a décor that combines tradition and whimsy, and now they and their families enjoy relaxing get-aways throughout the year. Sandra and her husband, David, were married on the front steps of the home in April of 1977. Photograph and information provided by David Jameson.

Pastor Percy Hughes (kneeling in front) and his congregation pose here in a 1940 photograph taken during Homecoming at Black Creek Baptist Church in Dovesville, Darlington County.

CROCK POT HASH
Contributed by John Waldrop

4 to 4 1/2	pounds of Boston butt roast
1 1/2 to 2	pounds of beef chuck roast
3	baking potatoes, peeled and diced
3	medium onions, peeled and diced

Seasonings (use only as a guide; adjust as preferred):

5	tablespoons of white vinegar
2	tablespoons of spicy brown mustard
1	tablespoon of red pepper flakes
2	teaspoons of cayenne pepper
4	tablespoons of tomato paste
1	stick of butter
2	tablespoons of Worcestershire sauce

salt and cracked black pepper to taste

Step 1: Rub both roasts with salt and cracked pepper, then place in the crock pot. Add the diced potatoes and onions, and fill the pot with hot water or stock and cover. Let it cook six to seven hours, until the meat falls apart. Keep an eye on the water level.

Step 2: Remove the meat from the pot and pull apart to allow it to cool. Next, remove the bone, fat, and connective tissue. Pull the meat apart in small pieces and chop it lightly (it can be ground up for a fine consistency). Break up the potatoes and onions in the pot with a potato masher. Return the meat to the pot. Add the butter and reduce heat to the lowest setting. Cook another six hours or until it is the consistency you like.

Step 3: Add the seasonings one at a time and taste as you go.

Step 4: Serve over white rice or white bread.

BARBECUED CHICKEN

When it comes to barbecue, pork is the primary meat chosen in the Palmetto State—but don't let that statistic mislead you. Poultry has claimed its rightful (and delicious!) place on the plates of South Carolinians, too.

The broiler—a young chicken raised for meat—is one of South Carolina's leading agricultural commodities. Naturally, some of the state's distinctive barbecue sauces and methods of cooking have been developed and fine-tuned as a result of the abundance and popularity of broilers, making for some finger-lickin' good barbecued chicken delights. Historically, chicken has been and is often cooked right alongside a pig or even on a separate, smaller pit, providing both nutritional diversity and a culinary diversion for cooks who stay up all night to roast a pig and their companions who stay up with them. And there are plenty of folks who prefer barbecued chicken to pork when given the choice. Whether the main meat is poultry or pork, many a South Carolina event centers around these mouth-watering smoked meats and a delectable array of sides.

The popularity of barbecued poultry became so broad that extension services around the nation began to produce educational circulars to aid consumers in preparing and barbecuing chicken. South Carolina had such a publication, published by Clemson University's Extension Service. The latest edition was edited by Clemson University Poultry Sciences professor Dr. John F. Welter, who earned his nickname, "The Chicken Man," as a result of his having barbecued thousands—literally—of chicken halves since the 1960s. Dr. John Welter's famous barbecued chicken has fed countless Southerners at school, athletic, church, community, fundraising, Clemson and special events for decades. The *Barns, Barbecue and Bales of Cotton* team is so pleased to feature "The Chicken Man" in this section of the book, as well as present a portion of the Extension Service's now-discontinued barbecued chicken circular.

We may never know why the chicken crossed the road, but we do know that many a South Carolinian has traveled many a mile down the road to enjoy South Carolina's very own chicken, barbecued to perfection.

BARBECUING CHICKEN

John Welter and Tom Stewart prepared the Barbecuing Chicken Bulletin *for Clemson University's Extension Service for more than twenty years. This bulletin was the most widely distributed of all Clemson's Extension bulletins. This information is reproduced with permission of the Extension Service from a 1970s version of the bulletin.*

EQUIPMENT

Have on hand all the necessary equipment and items you'll need for your chicken barbecue before you start to cook the chicken. Once the chicken becomes hot enough to start cooking, the chef or attendant should stay close to the grill until the meat is done. The chicken can burn while the cook is away, even if just for a few minutes.

- ❏ Grill
- ❏ Chickens (halved) weighing 2 to 2 1/2 pounds for whole chicken
- ❏ Salt
- ❏ Tongs for turning chicken
- ❏ Aluminum foil
- ❏ Barbecue sauce
- ❏ Brush for applying sauce
- ❏ Apron
- ❏ Gloves (heavy-duty cotton or leather)
- ❏ Small table or serving cart
- ❏ Paper towels
- ❏ Charcoal (for charcoal grills)—1 pound of briquettes per 2 pounds of whole chicken
- ❏ Odorless lighter fluid
- ❏ Can for starting fire (if using charcoal)—Make a starter can by cutting out the top and bottom of a 1-gallon tin can and using a can opener to puncture holes around the bottom.
- ❏ Matches and hot pads

STARTING THE FIRE ON A CHARCOAL GRILL

Remove the grill grate and place the starter can in the middle of the fire bowl. Pour two-thirds of the required briquettes into the can and raise it slightly to create a draft. Using a starter can decreases the time needed to produce a hot fire by as much as fifteen to twenty minutes. Pour on odorless lighter fluid and allow twenty minutes for the fluid to soak into the briquettes.

Replace the grill over the bowl. Lay chicken halves on the grill with the skin side up. Apply salt liberally to each half to adequately cover the skin. Leave the chicken in this position until the bony side is hot. This usually takes about twenty to thirty minutes. Do not let the chicken get too hot before turning, or it will stick to the grill. When the chicken is turned, add another liberal sprinkling of salt to the bony side of each half.

Add the remaining one-third of the charcoal briquettes when cooking is well underway (about fifteen to twenty minutes).

If you do not have a starter can, place two-thirds of the required briquettes in a pile in the middle of the bowl. Pour odorless lighter fluid over the pile, allowing adequate time for the fluid to soak into the briquettes, and then light the charcoal. When the charcoal has burned to a grayish color, spread the briquettes evenly over the bowl and add the remaining one-third of the required charcoal briquettes evenly over the hot coals. Following this procedure produces the right amount of heat to start the cooking. Chicken should never be placed on the grill until the briquettes have burned to a grayish color.

Use tongs instead of a fork to turn the chicken halves. Using a fork or other sharp-pointed instrument pierces the skin and meat and lets out the juices.

COOKING TIME

Allow at least two and a half hours to start the fire and complete the cooking. Take care to conserve all the heat possible using foil or covers to hold the heat over the chicken. One way to do this is to cover the portions of the grill not covered by the chicken with a sheet of aluminum foil or metal pan. A strip of aluminum can also be used between the grill and fire bowl to keep out the wind. Adjust the grill constantly to keep the chicken from burning, but do not raise it too far from the fire to slow down the cooking.

WHEN TO APPLY SAUCE

Do not begin basting with the sauce as soon as cooking starts. The sauce is wasted if it is applied while the excess moisture and fat are being cooked out of the chicken. During the early stage of cooking, considerable pressure is generated by the moisture and fat, and it is doubtful if any appreciable amount of sauce penetrates the skin and meat at this stage.

Apply the sauce during the last thirty minutes of cooking. During this time, turn the chicken several times and liberally apply the sauce after each turning.

BARBECUE SAUCES

Many barbecue sauces are available in retail stores. Most are general-purpose sauces and may not be as tasty on chicken as on other meats. One important thing to remember when considering a sauce for barbecued chicken is that a sauce containing a large amount of tomato sauce or catsup will cause the chicken to burn easily. Even slight burning may ruin the appearance.

Try the following homemade sauce the next time you barbecue chicken over the grill. This recipe has been used by members of the Clemson University Extension poultry staff in conducting hundreds of barbecue demonstrations throughout the state.

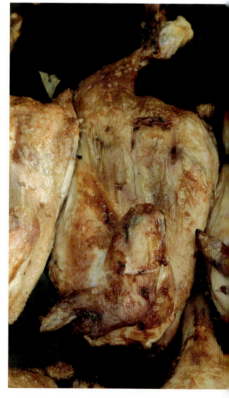

TOM STEWART'S BARBECUE SAUCE

1	quart of vinegar
1	pint of corn oil
4 1/2	ounces of mustard (1/2 of a 9-ounce jar)
1/4	bottle of onion salt
2 1/2	ounces of Worcestershire sauce (1/2 of a 5-ounce bottle)
1	cup of sugar
1/2	cup of salt
1/2	of a small bottle of tomato catsup
2	heaping teaspoons of black pepper

Mix together all ingredients thoroughly. No cooking or refrigeration is necessary. This recipe makes a 1/2-gallon of sauce, which is sufficient to barbecue 100 chicken halves or to supply the average family for the entire outdoor cooking season. It can also be used in preparing oven-barbecued chicken or on other meats.

If the Tom Stewart sauce doesn't suit your taste, try one of the following:

SAUCE NO. 1

1/2	cup of water
1 1/2	cups of vinegar
1/2	cup of corn oil or other vegetable oil
3	tablespoons of salt

Mix together all ingredients. Shake well. Requires no cooking or refrigeration. Makes 2 1/2 cups of sauce. This sauce may be sprayed on chicken with a pressure sprayer.

SAUCE NO. 2

1/2	cup of water
1/2	cup of vinegar
1/2	cup of corn oil or other vegetable oil
1	cup of catsup
3	tablespoons of salt
2	tablespoons of sugar
1	tablespoon of Worcestershire sauce
1	teaspoon of Tabasco sauce
1/2	teaspoon of black pepper
1	ground or finely chopped onion (well cooked before it is added to other ingredients)

Mix together all ingredients. Shake well. Requires no cooking. Makes 2 1/2 cups of sauce. Refrigerate unless used promptly.

TEST FOR DONENESS

Serving a well-cooked chicken is the most important part of the entire barbecuing process. Nobody likes a half-done piece of chicken. And there is no such thing as "rare" or "medium rare" chicken, as is the case with some other meats.

To test for doneness, hold the joint between the thigh and the drumstick firmly with the tongs. Grasp the exposed end of the drumstick bone with the other hand and turn. If the bone turns easily without undue pressure, the chicken can be considered done. If you do not plan to serve the chicken immediately, remove it from the grill and wrap it in aluminum foil or place it in an insulated container. The chicken will dry out rapidly and lose some of its tenderness and flavor if it is left on the fire.

PREPARING FOR LARGE BARBECUES

Chicken barbecues are popular for serving clubs and organizations where several hundred or several thousand people attend. Many organizations have found that putting on a chicken barbecue is one of the easiest, quickest and most profitable ways to make money for their treasury.

As with backyard barbecuing, be sure to have all equipment and supplies on hand before putting the chicken on to cook.

CONSTRUCTING PITS

Pits of any desired size can be made with cement blocks. If the pit is to be permanent, the cement blocks at one end should not be cemented together. In case more draft is needed, some of the blocks may be removed. If the pit is to be a temporary structure, the cement blocks can be temporarily stacked three high on top of one another.

Homemade wire grates can be made at a local welding shop. The grill shown in the photograph (right) is a convenient size for two people to handle. This size grill holds forty halves weighing from one to one and a half pounds each.

STARTING THE FIRE

To start the fire, place charcoal (two-thirds of the required amount) into several piles in the pit. Pour odorless charcoal lighter fluid on it and set it afire. After most of the briquettes have turned gray, spread them evenly over the bottom of the pit with a short-toothed rake. If a stiff breeze is blowing, do not add the remaining one-third of the briquettes until the cooking is well underway.

Each time you add briquettes, rake the bottom of the pit. If you want more heat to speed up the cooking process, rake the coals gently.

PIT COOKING

Put chicken halves on the grills as close together as possible, but do not overlap. Spacing them closely keeps the heat within the pit. Also cover that portion of the pit not covered by chicken with a piece of heavy

duty cardboard with no printing on it to keep the heat in and speed up the cooking.

While waiting for the charcoal to get hot enough, place the chicken on the grills. Then stack the loaded grills on top of one another, but not yet over the hot coals. When the briquettes have been spread, place all the grills over the heat at one time. Broadcast salt over the chicken halves.

You will need an extra grate to turn the chicken. To turn the chicken, two people should place the empty grill on top of each loaded grill in turn; then, by crossing their arms in front of their bodies, they can turn an entire grillful of chicken halves at one time.

Do not wait too long to turn the chicken the first time. If you wait too long, the chicken will stick to the grill. Broadcast salt over the bony side of each half and cover with corrugated paper to retain heat. Make a constant check of each grill to determine how often to turn the chicken to prevent burning.

Wait until the last thirty minutes of cooking before basting with the sauce. Use a mop or brush with a handle long enough to reach halfway across the grills.

SUGGESTED MENU AND SUPPLIES FOR SERVING BARBECUED CHICKEN

Number of People	10	50	100
Food Needed			
Rice	1 lb.	4 lb.	8 lb.
Gravy	1 qt.	1 gal.	2 gal.
Tossed salad	1 qt.	5 qt.	10 qt.
Slaw	1 qt.	5 qt.	10 qt.
Potato chips	1 lb.	4 lb.	8 lb.
Baked Beans	2 qt.	2 gal.	4 gal.
Sliced tomatoes	1 1/2 lb.	3 lb.	15 lb.
Mixed sweet pickles	1 pt.	2 qt.	1 gal.
Stuffed olives	1/2 pt.	1 qt.	1/2 gal.
Bread (regular-sized loaves)	1 loaf	3 loaves	6 loaves
Rolls	1 1/2 doz.	5 doz.	10 doz.
Coconut or apple pies	2 pies	8 pies	15 pies
Coffee, tea or lemonade	1 gal.	5 gal.	10 gal.
Coffee cream	1 pt.	2 qt.	3 qt.
Sugar	1/4 lb.	1 lb.	1 1/2 lb.
Ice cream	1 1/2 qt.	2 gal.	4 gal.
Milk, 1/2 pint	3	12	25
Chocolate milk, 1/2 pint	3	12	25
Ice water			
Supplies Needed			
Sectional plates, paper	12	60	125
Pie plates, paper	12	60	125
Coffee cups, paper	20	100	150
Spoons, plastic	25	100	200
Forks, plastic	12	60	125
Straws	12	48	100
Salt and pepper shakers	1 pair	3 pair	5 pair
Paper napkins (at least 2 per person)	24	100	250

SERVING THE MEAL

Have enough people on hand to serve each food item on the menu, rather than allowing the guests to help themselves. This eliminates waste and the chance of food items giving out before everyone is served. It also speeds up the serving time.

Depending on the size of the crowd expected, enough serving help should be available to complete the serving in fifteen to twenty minutes. Serving the ice water and drinks some distance from the main food line will avoid confusion and speed up the serving time.

CLEANING THE GRILLS

A simple, quick and easy way to clean the grills is to pour the charcoal into a pile across the pit. Stack all the grills over the charcoal, sprinkle the grill thoroughly with kerosene, ignite, and the grills will rapidly burn off. Wipe off the soot residue by rubbing the grills with old rags or paper.

JOHN WELTER, THE "CHICKEN MAN"
Written by Barbara T. Clark, longtime friend and neighbor of John Welter

For about as long as anyone around here can remember, John Finlay Welter has been barbecuing chicken—lots of chicken. For a single event, he has served anywhere from forty chickens to four thousand, and he's been doing it for more than fifty years. Though by his own admission he "retired from the business seven times in 2007 and five times in 2008," it doesn't appear that John Welter's last barbecue will be happening any time soon.

John grew up on a forty-acre cotton farm on Roper Mountain in Greenville County. According to John, it was the aspiration of every rural American family in the 1930s to own "a family farm with forty acres and a mule." For a time he lived in a log cabin, the one now labeled "Finlay Welter" at the Roper Mountain Science Center, while his parents were building their farmhouse.

Like many young people at that time, John was active in the 4-H Club. He decided to raise chickens and get involved in the production of eggs and other farm produce, which he sold at the "curb market" in Greenville. His business was so successful that it changed the nature of the family farm. When his father discovered how much money John was making, he gave up growing cotton and moved into the produce business himself.

Unfailingly resourceful, John took his local award-winning poultry project to the Twenty-fifth Anniversary 4-H Congress in Chicago. There his project earned him a scholarship of one hundred dollars a year for college. Coupled with the one-hundred-dollar-a-year scholarship he garnered from Sears Roebuck in its contest based on knowledge of agricultural practices, and supplemented by his ROTC earnings, John financed his next four years at Clemson University.

John Welter, "The Chicken Man," is pictured here (right) turning chicken halves at a barbecue before a Clemson University football game in the 1960s. Photograph contributed by Trent Allen.

With a degree in poultry science and considerable experience in the chicken business, John worked briefly at a farmers' cooperative for a county extension service and as manager of an egg production farm. He moved to Clemson in 1961 to manage the poultry center, the research end of the University's Poultry Science Department, and to attend graduate school. He settled his family in Clemson and, after graduate school, was invited to work for the Clemson University Extension poultry science staff. He later served as a district agent and as a poultry specialist for the state before retiring in 1988.

John Welter is shown here in 2007 barbecuing chicken on one of the barbecue pits at his Seneca home on Lake Hartwell.

Paralleling his professional career, for which he is well-known, is his barbecuing career, for which he might be even better-known. Promoting poultry in every form while educating people in the many uses of poultry products is a major focus of the extension service. So, as part of his job, John did demonstrations for 4-H clubs, civic groups, garden clubs, schools and other organizations. When the poultry science club cooked and sold chicken as a fundraiser at ball games, other groups quickly latched on to the idea. In fact, Boy Scout Troop 135, based at the First Presbyterian Church in Clemson, sponsored its first chicken dinner in the late 1960s and now holds the record—forty years—for the longest continuous run of an annual barbecue fundraiser.

As the popularity of outdoor cooking and of serving chicken at large gatherings burgeoned, John took over the barbecuing business from the extension service. His name became synonymous with barbecued chicken in the upstate and he regularly cooked chicken several times a week. The Welter children earned much of their college money helping at barbecues. Friends and neighbors were frequently commandeered to serve food and pour the tea. Many locals will remember eating, and perhaps helping serve, chicken at the annual July Fourth Festival at the Foothills Area Family YMCA.

While John fashioned a portable barbecue pit that he could carry around in his truck, he also built a huge concrete pit in his backyard. Those neighbors blessed with favorable winds remember the savory aromas wafting up from that pit. And it was not unusual for one of the Welter children to show up on a neighbor's doorstep with foil-wrapped half-chickens left over from that day's barbecue.

Since "everything poultry" has long been his byword, it's not surprising that John established a chicken-cooking contest through the 4-H Club. It began in South Carolina but soon spread nationwide. John delights in noting that state legislator Larry Martin was among the first contest winners. John also set up a contest for cooking turkeys on the grill, established a poultry judging team, and worked with the organization that seeks to eliminate serious diseases among poultry. Naturally he also barbecues pork, beef and turkey.

Eggs fall under the poultry umbrella as well, so in the early 1980s John branched out into the omelette arena. He chopped up anything one could possibly want in an omelette, cracked the eggs, and served up a made-to-order delicacy for each delighted guest.

Whether he's preparing omelettes or barbecued chicken, it is obvious that John Welter is in his element and totally comfortable in his own skin. Never ruffled or in a hurry, John's perennial smile and mischievously understated turn of phrase have endeared him *and* his barbecued chicken to everyone he meets.

Grain bins rise from the center of a maturing field of soybeans. Photograph by Larry Kemmerlin, South Carolina Farm Bureau Federation.

BALES OF COTTON— THE PRODUCTS OF SOUTH CAROLINA AGRICULTURE

By Rowland P. Alston Jr.

Throughout my career as an Extension agent for Clemson University and as the host of the South Carolina Educational Television program *Making it Grow!*, I have had the privilege of watching things grow and helping to make things grow. Over thirty years of experience has convinced me that the plants and animals that grace our state's landscape are as much a part of its fabric as the people who live here.

I monitor the seasons of the year by watching the rows and pastures around the state. The appearance of a fresh, crisp color of green on dark soil as wheat seedlings break forth signals the winter months. When I smell newly turned dirt; and see planters behind their tractors placing cotton, peanuts, soybeans, vegetables and other seeds beneath the sod; and notice the budding of fruit trees; and when I witness wobbly new calves frolicking and playing around their mothers, I know spring has arrived. Summer brings the maturation of what began as tiny little sprouts; and at this point in their growth, those with a trained eye can recognize what crop is in a field even when driving by at seventy miles per hour.

Then come late summer and autumn—harvest season in South Carolina. In late summer, the cornfields become brown and yield golden kernels. Soybeans turn from yellow to rust and their bounty flows from combine to wagon. Most noticeably, cotton fields lose their leaves and, in a good year at least, the white of the cotton makes it appear as though the snows have come early to South Carolina's countryside. These bolls of "snow" are collected into square mounds of cotton modules that wait to be taken to the gin like the giant snow drifts of the North. Seeing all that beautiful white "snow" reminds me that, in some ways, cotton is still king in South Carolina. It is certainly an emblem of South Carolina's rich agricultural heritage. Cotton fields, cotton gins, cotton-pickin' time, the South Carolina Cotton Trail, Cotton Festival, and the Cotton Museum in Bishopville, South Carolina—these are just a few of the phrases and symbols of this vital cash crop.

Though the production of cotton is not as plentiful as it once was, it is still a vibrant and wondrous row crop that has its place among our key agricultural commodities. When considering the major agricultural commodities produced in South Carolina, there is always room for debate. Our state's rich soils and various climates allow for a wide variety of production goals, and each producer considers his or her crop or breed to be the best. This is as it should be, for any producer worth their salt has put a great deal of thought into selecting what to grow on their plot of ground.

For the sake of this book, we have utilized the statistics from the USDA Agricultural Statistics Service as our guide. For the purpose of readability, space and continuity, we have combined and adjusted the commodities featured to provide as broad a picture as possible of the variety of agricultural goods South Carolina boasts. Suffice it to say, this is not an exhaustive exploration of South Carolina's commodities, but rather a depiction of the high-water marks during this time in our state's agricultural history.

And what of the organizations and institutions that aid and assist South Carolina's producers in their efforts to provide food and fiber for our state, nation and world? America truly has been the global leader in production agriculture with its development of the Land Grant College System and the related teaching, research and extension missions. Agricultural education programs for youth, such as Future Farmers of America and 4-H, enable us to nurture the most important crop of the future: young people who will pursue careers in agriculture and natural resources. Additionally, there are a variety of state, federal and grassroots agencies and organizations that provide support and services to ensure that America continues to produce a plentiful and safe supply of food and fiber. Each of these is also part of the story and we have selected a representative sampling of these organizations to showcase.

In the beginning and the end, it is all about "Making it Grow!" I am reminded of a phrase a fellow extension agent of mine used to share regularly to express the challenge faced by those who choose the profession of farming: "He who puts the seed beneath the sod and waits for it to raise a clod, he trusts in God!"

May we in South Carolina never violate this trust. Enjoy this glimpse into South Carolina's bales of cotton and bounty of crops.

This 1957 photograph by Elmer Turnage pictures students from Lower Richland High School participating in a field day demonstration of mulch-planting sponsored by Richland Soil Conservation District supervisors. Photograph provided by Sam McGregor.

BEEF CATTLE

Early English settlers in South Carolina recognized how well suited this new world region was for the production of cattle. The combination of the skills and knowledge they brought from England and the extensive experience of enslaved West Africans allowed for an expanding and successful cattle industry in South Carolina's early days. Over time, the vast plantations and ranches that initially dominated the trade began to decline. Large cattle herds belonging to wealthy plantation owners evolved into smaller herds that were part of family-owned and operated farms.

Since then, livestock production in South Carolina has experienced numerous transformations over the last two centuries to meet the needs of rural producers and in response to various social, political and economic chapters in the state's history. Through each season of change, the industry has successfully adapted as necessary and the cattle production industry in South Carolina has remained strong and stable.

Those who are devoted to animal husbandry are passionately bound to the associated lifestyle factors that surround the industry. There is a rhythm to the birth, growth and sale of a herd. The science and art of breeding and building quality stock and the struggles and triumphs of ranching create a unifying camaraderie among cattle producers. Additionally, the community of cattle producers engages in regular fellowship and establishes industry standards via an extensive network of local, state, regional and national shows. These shows provide the opportunity for a variety of standards for animals in the industry to be established and handling techniques to be perfected. Through the selection of show champions, they also allow for the marketing and promotion of animals and farms.

In the last decade, the pastures and fields of South Carolina have seen a rebirth of grazing livestock. From the coast to the foothills to the western counties at the foot of the Appalachian Mountains, cattle have made

A herd of Black Angus beef cattle grazes in a South Carolina field. Photograph by Larry Kemmerlin, South Carolina Farm Bureau Federation.

Beef cattle graze on a peaceful morning. Photograph by Larry Kemmerlin, South Carolina Farm Bureau Federation.

a comeback. Black Angus, Charolais, Herefords and numerous other breeds have become part of comprehensive farms or provided part-time work or retirement income for many South Carolinians.

According to the South Carolina Agricultural Statistics Office, South Carolina's cattle industry had 10,000 cattle farms with a total of 400,000 cattle and calves as of January 1, 2008. There were 197,000 beef cows and 18,000 milk cows in this inventory. The 2007 calf crop totaled 175,000 head, the same as in 2006 and down 3 percent from 2005. The calving rate for 2007 was 80.5 percent, up from 78.7 percent in 2006. South Carolina ranked thirty-ninth in the nation for all cattle and calves. Texas ranked first, Kansas second, Nebraska third and California fourth. The leading county in South Carolina was Anderson, followed by Laurens, Newberry, Saluda and York.

Replacement heifers on Guy Darby's farm in Chester enjoy a cool autumn morning. Photograph contributed by Sandy Poole.

To assist in maintaining a strong and viable presence in the state, livestock producers created the South Carolina Cattlemen's Association (SCCA). The association is owned, controlled, managed and funded by and for the cattle producers of the state. Its mission is to unite cattle producers to advance the economic, political and social interests of South Carolina's cattle industry and to increase the demand for beef and beef products within the state of South Carolina. The SCCA complements and furthers the efforts of more than twenty-five county or regional associations functioning around the state, and is a charter affiliate member of the National Cattlemen's Beef Association. The association's active Junior Member Association seeks to inspire and educate young people who are interested in cattle production.

Among the "firsts" at the 1971 Upper South Carolina State Fair were Charolais cattle, a new French breed, exhibited by 4-H and Future Farmers of America youths Jim Milford of Abbeville and Steve and Calvert Sherard of Calhoun Falls. Photograph contributed by Calvert Sherard.

Congress created the Beef Promotion and Research Act, the Beef Checkoff Program, when it passed the 1985 Farm Bill. The Beef Checkoff Program is a producer-funded marketing and research program designed to increase domestic and international demand for beef through promotion, research and new product development, and a variety of other marketing tools. The Cattlemen's Beef Board and United States Department of Agriculture oversee the collection and spending of Checkoff funds.

Cattle producers voted to make the Beef Checkoff Program mandatory in 1988, with 79 percent in favor of doing so. Producers asked that the program be built on the following tenets:

> *All producers and importers pay the equivalent of one dollar per head each time a beef animal is sold throughout its lifetime.*
> *One-half of the money collected by state beef councils—fifty cents of every dollar—is invested through the beef council in each state.*

All national Checkoff-funded programs are budgeted and evaluated by the Cattlemen's Beef Board, a stand-alone organization of Checkoff-paying producer volunteers.

Cattlemen's Beef Board producer members are nominated by producer organizations in their states and appointed by the U.S. Secretary of Agriculture.

Though markets continually shift and change and weather patterns will always impact forage production and grazing options, South Carolina cattle producers continue to produce quality beef products for the enjoyment of consumers. And the sight of a content herd of cattle grazing in a green pasture continues to afford South Carolinians an enduring and endearing image of rural South Carolina—one that reminds us of our state's esteemed agricultural heritage.

CORN

Corn has been a part of South Carolina's history since before the first settlers arrived. Native Americans were producing maize, a relative of modern corn, in South Carolina and throughout the American colonies long before the first English settlers set foot in the New World. Corn is a historical icon of survival and self-sufficiency. South Carolina experienced a heavy influx of colonists in the late 1600s. Those pioneers farmed for survival and corn was their major crop.

The primary benefit of growing corn in these early decades was its versatility—every part of the corn plant was usable. The

Stalks of corn are silhouetted against a beautiful Carolina sunset. Photograph by Larry Kemmerlin, South Carolina Farm Bureau Federation.

Sweet corn picked and ready to be shucked and eaten.

diet of the first South Carolinians included corn in some form at almost every meal. Fresh corn was eaten during the growing season. Syrups and spirits were produced by processing corn at various stages in its growth. Corn kernels were ground into meals of varying sizes and used to make baked goods, to coat meats prior to cooking and to make the delightful Southern staple: grits. Corn kernels, cobs, fodder and leaves were also used to feed livestock.

Corn being harvested. Photograph by Larry Kemmerlin, South Carolina Farm Bureau Federation.

Corn provided both sustenance and independence to South Carolinians through many difficult economic and political seasons. A family that maintained a corn crop could provide for their own needs and usually sell or barter corn or products made from corn for extra cash or necessary staples. The versatile corn plant even supplied a family's leisure needs in the form of corncob pipes and cob and husk dolls.

In the years leading up to the Civil War, corn production increased steadily as markets developed and expanded. But the war and subsequent Reconstruction period devastated production on a large scale. It was not until 1891 that corn production returned to its pre–war levels. In the last century, the corn production levels rose and fell based on market need, technological advances and the prominence of other crops, such as cotton and soybeans. Breeding advances and biotechnological advances have enabled farmers to produce much more corn on fewer acres.

In 2007, South Carolina farmers harvested 370,000 acres of grain corn, with each acre producing an average of one hundred bushels. With this total harvest of thirty-seven million bushels of corn, South Carolina is ranked twenty-sixth in the United States in corn production. Clarendon, Lee, Sumter and Orangeburg counties lead the state in corn production.

Edgefield County farmer Gregg Thomas harvests corn with his John Deere 6620 in late October of 2006 at Thomas Farms in Johnston.

To provide oversight and direction to promote and facilitate the production of corn in the state, producers combined their efforts with soybean producers. The South Carolina Corn and Soybean Association (SCCSA) is a membership organization involved in policy-making and lobbying. SCCSA is an affiliate of the American Soybean Association (ASA) and the National Corn Growers Association (NCGA). None of the Checkoff funds they receive may be used for political purposes. As with other commodity groups, members of SCCSA engage in and promote activities and programs intended to sustain the viability of corn production in South Carolina and respond to the needs of its membership.

COTTON

Often referred to as South Carolina's "Agricultural King," cotton was introduced to South Carolina by the first European settlers to arrive. In fact, settlers who didn't have the money to pay their way to America gained passage by agreeing to send two hundred pounds of cotton back to Europe within two years of arriving in the New World. This incentive helped cotton to immediately gain prominence as a cash crop in South Carolina.

Currently, harvested cotton is dumped in to a Cotton Module Press in the field that is retrieved by special trucks and then unloaded for the ginning process. Photograph by Minnie Miller.

Cotton production increased through the plantation system and the first major export of cotton to England occurred in 1764. What was known as Sea Island Cotton was produced in South Carolina, Georgia and Florida in the early nineteenth century and became well-known as the finest of cotton crops. Sea Island Cotton had long, fine, strong fibers and was greatly desired by the mills. South Carolina cotton producers enjoyed continued growth and wealth as production techniques and technology improvements led to higher and higher yields and more efficient and effective processing. Cotton became "king" in South Carolina.

The Civil War years brought embargoes, natural resource and infrastructure destruction, political and economic turmoil, and a loss of active producers in South Carolina. These issues, along with numerous other historical shifts, had a significant impact on "King Cotton." Following the problems of those decades, the boll weevil, a small beetle that feeds on cotton buds and flowers, invaded South Carolina. Thought to be native to Central America, the boll weevil migrated into the United States from Mexico in the late nineteenth century, devastating the cotton industry. By the time World War I began, cotton production in South Carolina was suffering drastically.

Since then, however, cotton has made a comeback. Numerous scientific and production advances have enabled cotton to reassert its leadership among South Carolina's agricultural cash commodities. New discoveries and advances in plant breeding, mechanization, irrigation, pest control and processing have allowed South Carolina and other states to improve cotton yields.

There are two varieties of cotton best suited for cultivation in South Carolina—Sea Island Cotton and Upland Cotton. Sea Island Cotton was the first cotton variety to achieve commercial success in South Carolina. It was grown near the coast in loose, sandy soil. Its silky fibers separated easily from the seeds and it was used mainly for delicate fabrics.

Upland Cotton is the main type of cotton grown in South Carolina. Upland Cotton became commercially significant with the invention of the modern cotton gin in the 1790s by American inventor Eli Whitney, which mechanized the cleaning of cotton. The cotton gin was granted a patent in 1794 and from the time it was introduced until around 1860, the cotton gin had a greater impact on the South than any other invention. Before the cotton gin's invention, it took a worker an entire day to remove enough seeds by hand to make one pound of lint cotton. The cotton gin revolutionized the process of cleaning and separating the fiber from the seeds. As a result, vast areas of land were converted into cotton plantations and there was a massive growth in cotton production throughout the South. South Carolina was no exception.

Before the advent of modules for holding cotton prior to ginning, wagons were seen all across the countryside during cotton-picking season, similar to this one from a former cotton gin in Mayesville, South Carolina.

Then in 1948 came the mechanical cotton picker, which automated cotton harvesting and transformed the way cotton farms operated. Throughout the nineteenth century, cotton had been planted and harvested with plows, hoes and strong backs, and little progress was made in farm mechanization. With the introduction of the mechanical cotton picker, all that changed. Even though the first mechanical cotton pickers could only harvest a row of cotton at a time, they replaced many human workers.

In the second half of the twentieth century, South Carolina's inner coastal plains became the primary area for the state's cotton production. This remains true today, with the top ten cotton-producing counties in South Carolina being Calhoun, Darlington, Dillon, Dorchester, Florence, Hampton, Lee, Marlboro, Orangeburg and Williamsburg, according to the latest statistics from the United States Department of Agriculture's National Agricultural Statistics Service. These statistics also indicate that 344,000 bales of cotton are harvested annually on 266,000 planted acres.

Cotton farmer Blain Player of Lee County examines cottonseeds with a local elementary school student after they have been ginned. Photograph contributed by Kirby Player.

It is not only the growth and production of cotton that is part of South Carolina's heritage. The ginning of cotton is also a vital part of the statewide rural community. In years past, cotton gins could be found at small rural community crossroads throughout the state. These gins sent cotton to the numerous textile mills all over the South. Today, there are nearly thirty cotton gins operating in South Carolina with varying activity.

Miss Ethel Robinson of New York City took special courses at Converse College in Spartanburg and is shown here in 1942 picking cotton, a novel experience for her.

One bale of cotton weighs about 480 pounds and it takes one bale of cotton to produce each of the following:

249 bed sheets
2,104 boxer shorts
3,085 diapers
2,419 men's briefs
1,265 pillowcases
690 terry bath towels
21,960 women's handkerchiefs
409 men's sport shirts
6,436 women's knit briefs
215 pairs of denim jeans
4,321 mid-calf socks
1,217 T-shirts
765 men's dress shirts
313,600 hundred-dollar bills

The cotton industry has created a variety of self-governing organizations to ensure its continued success. Two of the key organizations are the National Cotton Council of America and the Cotton Board.

The mission of the National Cotton Council of America is to ensure that all United States cotton industry segments have the ability to compete effectively and profitably in the raw cotton, oilseed and United States-manufactured product markets at home and abroad. The council serves as the central forum for consensus building among producers, ginners, warehousers, merchants, cottonseed processors and dealers, cooperatives and textile manufacturers. The organization is the unifying force in working with the government to ensure that the cotton industry's interests are considered.

Based in Memphis, Tennessee, the Cotton Board is the oversight and administrative arm of the Cotton Research and Promotion Program rep-

This late 1800s Connor Plantation cotton gin, restored by James A. Dantzler, is housed in the renovated original gin house inside the Elloree Heritage Museum in Orangeburg County. Photograph and information contributed by Mrs. Jim Ulmer.

resenting United States Upland Cotton. To fund the program, the Cotton Board collects a per-bale assessment on all Upland Cotton harvested and ginned in the United States, as well as an importer assessment for all Upland Cotton products imported into the country. To conduct the program, the board contracts with Cotton Incorporated to carry out the actual research and promotion activities for American producers and importers of cotton. While Cotton Incorporated is consumer- and trade-focused, it is a charged function of the Cotton Board's mission to keep United States producers and importers of cotton informed on the innovative developments stemming from the Cotton Research and Promotion Program.

Anyone who has seen a boll-laden field of fully opened cotton understands the sense of wonder and magic such a sight inspires. This snowy fiber is transformed into countless useful products. Since South Carolina was settled, cotton has been a part of its rich and colorful heritage—and it appears that South Carolina will long continue to be the blessed "Land of Cotton!"

DAIRY

South Carolina dairy farmers provide consumers daily with "Milk, Nature's Most Nearly Perfect Food." Milk is the official state beverage of South Carolina, and dairy farms can be found in nineteen of the state's forty-six counties. The dairy industry is an important sector of agriculture in South Carolina. In 2006, the South Carolina dairy industry generated an estimated $177.9 million in economic activity.

Milk has long been a popular beverage, not only for its flavor, but because of its unique nutritional package. Milk is one of the best sources of calcium available, and provides high-quality protein, vitamins and other minerals. Other delicious dairy products made from milk include cheese, yogurt, ice cream, butter and cream.

A pasteurizing plant at Laurinton Dairy in 1950. Pasteurization is one innovation that contributed significantly to making milk a healthy and commercially viable product. Photograph contributed by Sam McGregor.

Cows of Laurinton Dairy Farm graze on rye grass and crimson clover in 1949. Photograph contributed by Sam McGregor.

A Jersey cow at the Milky Way Farm in Starr takes a break from grazing to gaze at the camera. Photograph contributed by Stephanie Phillips.

What many folks think of as the "typical" dairy cow is white with black spots. Photograph by Larry Kemmerlin, South Carolina Farm Bureau Federation.

Little is known about the earliest period of dairy farming in South Carolina because acquiring milk was primarily an individual family enterprise. A family that produced excess dairy products sold or traded the products to neighbors. Eventually, some farmers acquired an extra dairy cow or two for the purpose of producing dairy products to sell. As demand grew, herds increased in size.

As the state's population moved from farms to towns and cities, it became necessary to mass-produce milk, as well as improve its quality. Significant inventions, such as commercial milk bottles, milking machines, pasteurization equipment, refrigerated milk tanks and automatic bottling machines, contributed to making milk a healthy and commercially viable product. Over time, milking equipment, processing equipment, packaging equipment and milk transportation systems were greatly improved. Plastic milk containers became available in 1964, forever changing the packaging of milk.

South Carolina has four commercial milk processing plants, located in Charleston, Florence, North Charleston and Spartanburg; and five farmer-operated milk processing plants located in Calhoun, Edgefield, Greenville, Lexington and Oconee counties.

Today's South Carolina dairy farmers use modern management practices and tools, including Dairy Herd Improvement computer records, artificial insemination, embryo transfer, forage testing, ration formulation and many more effective programs. South Carolina dairy farmers are excellent managers of cattle, crops, facilities and labor, and dairy farms include both intensive production systems and pasture-based systems.

Although dairy producers in South Carolina are some of the best herd managers in the Southeast, the number of dairy farms and cows has decreased. In 1950, there were 1,430 dairy farms in South Carolina with more than 158,000 cows. By 1990, the number had decreased to 222 dairy farms milking 40,000 cows. In 2009, there are 86 dairy farms milking approximately 18,000 cows.

Although the number of dairy farms in the state has declined, milk production per cow has dramatically increased from 3,549 pounds per cow in 1945 to 17,889 pounds per cow in 2007, an increase of 504 percent.

South Carolina dairy producers are on the threshold of some of the most dynamic technological changes in history. Technologies such as radio frequency identification, sexed semen, genomic testing and robotics will continue to impact this industry. The use of new technologies will depend on the individual dairy farmer's management skills and the profit opportunities a new practice offers.

Being a South Carolina dairy farmer requires a lot of care. They care for their cows and their land and they care about the product they produce. They take great pride knowing that dairy foods help consumers maintain a healthy lifestyle.

ORNAMENTAL HORTICULTURE AND THE GREEN INDUSTRY

Mums and magnolias. Poinsettias and pansies. Lush green lawns. Annuals and perennials that offer a kaleidoscope of color. Shrubs in all shapes and sizes. All of these wonderful plants and more are a part of South Carolina's vast and continually growing ornamental horticulture and green industry. Whether it is a bowl of blooming bulbs given to a sick friend or plants used to stabilize the ground and prevent erosion, ornamental plants fill our lives with purpose and pleasure. They make our state beautiful, enriching our daily lives, attracting tourists and increasing traffic at businesses.

Clemson University's Botanical Gardens is home to a multitude of local flora. This beautiful Clemson orange bloom was captured by Karen Creel on a stroll through the gardens.

A field of bright purple perennials blooms at a nursery in the Edgefield area. Photograph provided by Steve Jeffers.

A tree is harvested at an upstate tree production nursery. Photograph contributed by Steve Jeffers.

Growers in South Carolina produce annuals, perennials, trees and shrubs by both container and balled and burlapped methods. They produce turf grass, herbs, native plants, bulbs and plants for re-nourishing the state's coast. Some growers specialize in one type of plant, while others offer a huge selection. South Carolina's excellent growing climate allows for the successful production of a vast number of plant varieties, many of which are shipped to customers throughout the Southeast and beyond.

In South Carolina, as well as most other Southern states, ornamental horticulture is one of the top three agricultural cash crops. South Carolina's ample interstate system and its climate, along with the availability of land, contribute to the success of the industry. This industry provides employment for a large number of South Carolina residents, employing growers, propagators, plant specialists, farm workers, office workers and truck drivers. Additionally, the industry supports an even farther-reaching job palette of landscape contractors, irrigation specialists, landscape designers, garden center workers, researchers and educators. The economic impact of the industry is enjoyed across the state with every county benefiting to some degree.

South Carolina has several claims to fame related to the ornamental horticulture and green industry. The first camellias brought to America are planted at Middleton Place Plantation in Charleston. South Carolina statesman Joel Poinsett introduced poinsettias to America, bringing them from Mexico. One reason South Carolina is called the Palmetto State is because palmetto tree logs were used to build military forts—their rubbery trunks simply absorbed enemy cannon balls rather than being destroyed by them. Johns Island is home to the "Angel Oak," which is believed to be more than 1,400 years old and is consid-

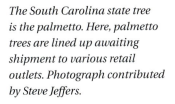

The South Carolina state tree is the palmetto. Here, palmetto trees are lined up awaiting shipment to various retail outlets. Photograph contributed by Steve Jeffers.

ered the oldest thing, living or man-made, east of the Mississippi River. Ornamentals, in all their various forms, are a part of our history, our survival and our celebrations.

The ornamental horticulture industry has shown tremendous growth in the last fifty years, and is expected to continue to thrive. As the financial status of American families has grown, so has their desire for beautiful outdoor living spaces. Public gardens, universities and associations have made great efforts to provide gardening information to consumers. The number of television shows with gardening themes has grown considerably. Businesses and industries of all types have learned that well-landscaped entryways, parking areas and lawns are good for both business and employee satisfaction and well-being. Medical research has shown that hospital patients who have a view of trees or a garden recover more quickly than those with unattractive views. Horticulture therapy is used with troubled youth and in the prison system.

PEACHES

What would summer be like without sweet, juicy South Carolina peaches? It wouldn't be summer at all—at least not as residents of the Palmetto State know it. Generations of South Carolinians have enjoyed this delicious fruit as one of summer's most special treats. Fittingly, the peach was designated South Carolina's state fruit in 1984.

Peaches have been an important crop in South Carolina since the early 1800s and South Carolina's typical annual production is currently around two hundred million pounds. But peaches haven't always been grown and enjoyed here. Long before South Carolina was a state, in the 1500s or earlier, not a single peach tree ex-

A plump, juicy peach hanging from a tree is an iconic image of South Carolina agriculture and South Carolina life. Photograph by Larry Kemmerlin, South Carolina Farm Bureau Federation.

Peach blossoms are as beautiful to the eyes as the fruit is to the taste buds. Photograph by Larry Kemmerlin, South Carolina Farm Bureau Federation.

isted anywhere in North America. Peaches are native to China and were initially considered an exotic plant when the Spaniards introduced them to North America in the 1600s.

Over the last century, peach production in the southeastern United States has experienced periods of great expansion and profitability, as well as periods of contraction and peril. The industry experienced great expansion in the late 1800s, when the advent of refrigerated rail cars tremendously increased the marketing opportunity for Southeastern peaches. Peach growers, however, have suffered major setbacks, as well, for various reasons, including (1) Armillaria root rot disease; (2) peach tree short life, which is characterized by the sudden collapse and death of young peach trees; and (3) significant urban encroachment during the last two decades, which has resulted in many thousands of acres of formerly good peach growing land being forced out of production. Additionally, spring freezes in 1996 and 2007 nearly destroyed the entire Southeastern peach crop. But despite the setbacks, the peach continues to be a highly sought-after summer fruit and one that still can be very profitable to grow.

Spencer McLeod reaches into the peach bin at McLeod Farms in McBee, South Carolina. Photograph contributed by John Parris.

A historic rivalry exists between South Carolina and Georgia—both claim to be the "peachiest" state. Georgia uses the slogan, "The Peach State," while South Carolina has adopted the slogan, "The Tastier Peach State." In fact, South Carolina typically produces more peaches each year than Georgia. At last estimate, South Carolina's seventeen thousand acres of peaches exceeded Georgia's fifteen thousand acres, and South Carolina is currently the second-highest peach-producing state in the country. To keep us humble, however, it should be noted that South Carolina's peach production is dwarfed by California, which reports around ninety thousand acres of peaches. And to keep California humble, China has approximately 1.4 million acres of peaches, which accounts for 45 percent of the peaches produced in the entire world.

South Carolina peaches are sold as fresh fruit, as well as processed into many value-added products. Roadside and farmers markets typically feature "tree-ripened" fruits that are mature and ready to eat. These are picked from the tree and immediately sold by the basket or bag. They may be only hours off the tree when purchased. They are highly aromatic, soft to the touch, and have a taste that is deliciously sweet with a hint of acidity. Although peaches are often associated with going to the beach or family barbecues on the Fourth of July, the South Carolina peach season actually runs from early May until mid-September, about eighteen weeks.

Peaches destined for out-of-state markets are picked at a less mature stage then those sold locally. These peaches are cooled to 32 degrees Fahrenheit, packaged by size, placed in half-bushel boxes and shipped in large refrigerated trucks. They continue to ripen when they reach their final destination, remaining high in quality.

Those peaches not sold along South Carolina's roads or shipped to other locations are processed into other products. For example, some peaches are specifically grown to make baby food, while others are cultivated for jams, preserves, canned peaches, salsa, cider and ice cream.

Grower innovations over the last decade are many. More efficient irrigation practices use micro-sprinklers under the trees. Wind machines are used to limit cold damage, and high-density systems improve production efficiency. Specialty and nontraditional cultivars are being developed and promoted to niche markets. New products include white-fleshed peaches and nectarines, which are popular in Asian markets, as well as sub-acid yellow-fleshed peaches, which are high in sugar, low in acid and might be classified as "honey" peaches. Attempts have also been made to grow the genetic mutant "flat" or "donut" peaches, but these crops suffer from disease problems and remain difficult to grow at this point.

Most peach farms in South Carolina are family-owned operations, some of which have been in the same family for nearly one hundred years. They rely heavily on Hispanic laborers, who work in the state legally through the federal government's H-2A guest farmworker program. Without this skilled and hardworking labor force, the South Carolina peach industry as we know it would collapse. Guest farmworkers come primarily from Mexico and often work in South Carolina for eight to ten months a year. South Carolina farmers provide them with transportation, housing and excellent wages. In total, the more than fifty-million-dollar peach industry provides many permanent and temporary jobs vital to the state's rural economy.

A peach orchard in full bloom.

The South Carolina Peach Council consists of peach growers throughout the state and advisors from Clemson University. The council raises funds each year through an annual auction and update and uses the funds to support research projects aimed at solving grower problems and to promote the industry. The council works closely with the South Carolina Department of Agriculture, whose current slogan is "Nothing's Fresher. Nothing's Finer." This certainly applies to South Carolina's signature fruit—the peach.

POULTRY

There may be no clear answer to the question, "Which came first, the chicken or the egg?" but there is a definite answer to the question, "Which agricultural commodity leads the state consistently in cash sales receipts?" The answer is poultry—specifically broilers. The Palmetto State is a leading poultry producer and the poultry industry in South Carolina involves the production of chicken, turkey, eggs and a variety of other unique birds such as quail, pigeons and ostriches.

The South Carolina poultry industry represents 40 percent of all agriculture in the state and 80 percent of all animal agriculture. The industry has a significant impact on the economy of South Carolina. Sales receipts total $1.5 billion annually and production occurs throughout the state, positively impacting residents all over the Palmetto State.

Poultry production in South Carolina consists of a variety of products. The South Carolina egg industry produces an average of 68.5 million dozens of eggs from an average of 5.5 million layers. South Carolina is ranked seventeenth in the nation in egg production. Within the state, Newberry County ranks first, followed by Kershaw, Darlington, Saluda and Lexington counties.

The South Carolina broiler sector averages 235 million broilers each year, which equates to about 1.5 billion pounds. Lexington, Aiken, Oconee, Clarendon and Sumter are the leading broiler-producing counties. South Carolina ranks thirteenth in the nation in broiler production.

Kershaw County leads in the production of turkeys, followed by Lancaster, Chesterfield, Lee and Newberry counties. About ten million turkeys, some 335 million pounds, are raised in South Carolina each year. South Carolina ranks eighth in the nation—its highest poultry production ranking—in turkey production.

The other poultry industries in South Carolina include quail, pigeon, pousson and squab. Combined they produce more than 6.5 million birds annually, an estimated twenty million pounds. Most are raised in or close to Sumter County.

The South Carolina egg industry produces an average of 68.5 million dozens of eggs from an average of 5.5 million layers. South Carolina is ranked seventeenth in the nation in egg production. Photograph by Larry Kemmerlin, South Carolina Farm Bureau Federation.

Chickens feed on grain from a communal feeder. Photograph by Larry Kemmerlin, South Carolina Farm Bureau Federation.

The approximate number of jobs generated by South Carolina's poultry industry is 7,500. This number reflects employees of poultry companies and does not include allied jobs generated in connection with the poultry industry, such as refrigerated truck drivers, paper box and egg carton producers, rendering and construction company employees, etc. The jobs and products produced by the poultry industry contribute significantly to South Carolina's economy.

The South Carolina Poultry Federation was formed in 1987 and has served as the voice of the South Carolina poultry industry since then. The federation represents producers and processors of turkey, chicken, quail, squab and egg products, and provides a united voice for the industry in communicating with the government, the media and the public. The mission of the federation is to preserve, promote and protect the activities that bring value to the stakeholders of the poultry industry in the state of South Carolina.

Federation membership consists of growers, producers, industry employees, allied industry suppliers and "main street" businesses that recognize the importance of poultry to the state's economy. Officers, directors and committee members represent all segments of the poultry industry and serve without compensation, giving freely of their time and talents to keep South Carolina's poultry industry competitive. In addition to representatives from all areas of the poultry industry and allied industries, representatives from Clemson University and the South Carolina commissioner of agriculture serve as ex officio (non-voting) board members.

About ten million turkeys, some 335 million pounds, are raised in South Carolina each year. Photograph by Larry Kemmerlin, South Carolina Farm Bureau Federation.

There is no question that the South Carolina poultry industry has played and will continue to play an important role in providing opportunity and income for producers in rural South Carolina. The next time you eat a scrambled egg, bite into a juicy, warm piece of fried chicken or carve a mouth-watering turkey for Thanksgiving, you just might be tasting the bounty of South Carolina's poultry producers.

SOYBEANS

The soybean is often called the "miracle crop" because it provides most of the world's protein and oil. Soybean plants are legumes, similar to beans, peas, clover, alfalfa and peanuts. Legumes have seed pods as fruit and nodules on their roots containing bacteria that convert nitrogen from the air into usable forms for the plant.

Chinese farmers planted soybeans more than five thousand years ago. Records indicate that Chinese soybean varieties were first planted in the English colonies around 1765 by Mr. Samuel Bowen near Savannah, Georgia, in order to manufacture soy sauce and vermicelli, or soy sprouts. In the 1800s, farmers began to grow soybeans as forage for cattle. Later,

When they are ready to be harvested, soybeans have a brown, dry appearance. Photograph by Larry Kemmerlin, South Carolina Farm Bureau Federation.

Civil War soldiers used soybeans to brew a type of "coffee" when real coffee was scarce.

From 1924 to 1931, several United States Department of Agriculture (USDA) scientists took two major exploration trips to collect soybean germplasm from China, Japan and Korea. As a result, public and private soybean breeders developed new and improved cultivars, which was the greatest contributing factor to the increase in United States soybean production.

Prior to World War II, the United States imported 40 percent of its edible fats and oils. The war placed this supply in jeopardy and processors turned to soybean oil instead. During the 1950s, the acreage devoted to planting soybeans in South Carolina expanded tremendously. Production and acreage continued to increase in the state, topping out at more than 1.8 million acres and nearly forty million bushels in 1982. For a number of reasons, including price, inputs, urban sprawl, farm policy, fewer farmers, other crops and an increase in technology and efficiency, soybean acreage has decreased since then, but has remained stable at around half a million acres since 1990. In 2008, it is estimated that there were 520,000 soybean acres harvested for a total production of more than fourteen million bushels.

The soybeans pictured here are young soybeans, just beginning to grow. Photograph by Larry Kemmerlin, South Carolina Farm Bureau Federation.

There are thirteen different soybean Maturity Groups (MGs), which are based upon the time flowers appear on a plant. South Carolina farmers grow mostly indeterminate varieties in MG V, VI, VII and VIII, typically planting between mid-May and late June and harvesting the crop in November and December. A mature soybean plant has around sixty to eighty pods and each pod usually contains three beans. Harvest begins when seed moisture levels reach an ideal moisture level, and timely harvest is crucial to maximize both yield and quality. Farmers use a combine to harvest soybeans and then either store them in bins or haul them directly to a first purchaser. Advancements in biotechnology, genetically improved varieties, pesticides, machinery and precision agriculture have allowed producers more efficient and effective management options. These also allow farmers to engage in more conservation practices that reduce the environmental impacts of producing a crop.

In processing, soybeans are cleaned, cracked, de-hulled and rolled into flakes. This ruptures the oil cells for efficient extraction to separate the hull, oil and meal components. Soy hulls are processed into cereal and snacks for human consumption and can also be used as filler in cattle feed. Soybean oil is used primarily in the food industry in products like margarine, salad dressing and cooking oils. Soybeans are the highest natural source of dietary fiber and contain eight essential amino acids necessary for human nutrition but not produced naturally by the human body. Research and numerous studies have confirmed the health benefits of soy, and simply glancing around the grocery store proves that soy foods are growing exponentially in popularity.

While the protein-rich flakes can be made into a number of edible products, the majority of soybean meal becomes animal feed. Those engaged in animal agriculture are the soybean farmer's number-one customers, accounting for more than 96 percent of the domestic use of soybeans.

Soybean oil has other important industrial uses and is found in plastics, foam and insulation, and is the primary feedstock in biodiesel fuel. There are commercial soy-based biodiesel producers, as well as retail locations that sell the product, right here in South Carolina. Soybeans can go from the field to the fuel tank without ever leaving the state.

Brothers Gregg and Kelly Thomas work together to harvest soybeans as quickly as possible so they can ready the land for planting grain.

The South Carolina Soybean Board (SCSB) is a farmer-led group that oversees the investment of Soybean Checkoff dollars on behalf of all South Carolina soybean farmers. The Soybean Checkoff is supported entirely by soybean farmers who make individual contributions of 0.5 percent of the market price per bushel sold each season. The efforts of the Checkoff are directed at the state level by the SCSB and at the national level by the United Soybean Board (USB). The SCSB is made up of twelve farmer-directors, nominated by their peers, and the USB is composed of sixty-eight volunteer farmer-leaders nominated by their state-level Checkoff organizations. Checkoff funds are invested in research, promotion and education in the areas of animal utilization, human utilization, industrial utilization, industry relations, market access and supply. As stipulated in the Soybean Promotion, Research and Consumer Information Act, the United States Department of Agriculture's Agricultural Marketing Service has oversight responsibilities for USB and the Soybean Checkoff.

A golden setting sun peaks out from behind a large stalk of tobacco. Photograph by Larry Kemmerlin, South Carolina Farm Bureau Federation.

TOBACCO

Adapted from: "South Carolina's Tobacco Heritage," The Tobacco Institute, Washington, D.C.

Tobacco seeds were carried into the Carolina territory more than three hundred years ago by English colonists arriving from Barbados. For two hundred years after its introduction, tobacco—the golden leaf—prospered in South Carolina.

There were setbacks, of course. When the modern cotton gin was invented in the 1790s, many planters turned their attention from tobacco to cotton, but bumper crops of cotton depressed prices and the emerging boll weevil drove growers back to tobacco. Then the Civil War and ensuing Reconstruction brought all of South Carolina's agriculture to a halt.

By the end of the nineteenth century, however, South Carolinians were again growing large quantities of tobacco. By then they were growing a variety known as bright, because the leaf turned lemon yellow during curing. Demand grew for this lighter, finer leaf and it sold at premium prices. Post-war tobacco cultivation continued to increase and South Carolina introduced regular warehouse and inspection procedures. Markets opened in Cheraw, Columbia, Charleston, Camden and Beaufort. Much of South Carolina's tobacco was sent to Virginia and North Carolina, where processing and manufacturing centers were evolving. Initially, there were attempts to manufacture tobacco products in South Carolina, but this boom was short-lived as competition from Virginia and North Carolina proved too strong for the South Carolinians.

W. H. Daniel, a Confederate soldier imprisoned in New York, returned to North Carolina and then pioneered the development of bright tobacco

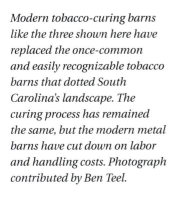

Modern tobacco-curing barns like the three shown here have replaced the once-common and easily recognizable tobacco barns that dotted South Carolina's landscape. The curing process has remained the same, but the modern metal barns have cut down on labor and handling costs. Photograph contributed by Ben Teel.

in South Carolina's northeast Pee Dee area. Daniel founded the state's first tobacco warehouse in Mullins, called Planters Warehouse, as well as a redrying plant. Bright tobacco culture caught on quickly in the Northeastern counties of Horry, Marion, Florence, Williamsburg, Darlington, Sumter and Clarendon. Tobacco later expanded into Chesterfield, Dillon, Georgetown and Lee counties. Another tobacco pioneer was Frank M. Rogers, who started a small patch in Florence County in 1882.

Tobacco holds a paramount position in South Carolina's economy and makes a considerable contribution to the Palmetto State in jobs and in income and tax revenues. The major form of tobacco produced in South Carolina is officially classified by the United States Department of Agriculture as Type 13. This production is concentrated in the Pee Dee area of the state. Together, South Carolina and southeastern North Carolina make up what is called the Flue-cured Border Belt. Flue-cured is the most extensively grown tobacco in the United States and is the principal export tobacco. The leaf is yellow to orange, thin to medium-bodied, and mild in flavor. Its name comes from the metal flues used in early curing barns.

In the old days, Palmetto State tobacco farmers sowed tiny seeds, approximately 450,000 to the ounce, between December and March. An ounce of seeds produced enough plants for four to five acres. These beds were sown outside and covered with plastic canvas and the seeds germinated in two to three weeks.

Since the early 1990s, tobacco transplants have been grown in greenhouses in a plant-tray system. Between early April and mid-May, the young plants are transplanted into the field. The entire process takes about eight weeks from planting to transplanting in the field.

Flue-cured tobacco grows best in fertile soils. The flowers are removed from the plants, enabling their leaves to draw more nutrients and grow larger and thicker. Later, buds, or "suckers," once tediously removed by hand, are eliminated with chemical sprays. The plants are ripe and ready for harvesting when their green leaves fade and turn a dull yel-

This 1963 photograph shows William Quincy Todd holding his granddaughter, Lenora Todd, amid a field of Hicks Tobacco. Hicks Tobacco topped out at around five feet and each planting yielded six crops. Mr. Todd was a sharecropper on the Jones farm and sold his tobacco crop at the Carmichael Warehouse in Mullins for about sixty cents per pound for the highest grade. Photograph and information contributed by Lenora Todd Weatherly, who credits "Granddaddy" with having passed along his love of plants and dirt to her.

Workers putting racks of tobacco into curing barns at the Hebron Community in Williamsburg County. Photograph and information contributed by Douglas M. Edgeworth.

lowish-green. Beginning at the bottom of the plant, tobacco is harvested three or four times from June to early September.

In the old days, leaves were hung from sticks in conventional barns and either oil-burning heaters or open-flame gas heaters were used to dry the tobacco. Later, timesaving practices were introduced in the form of bulk barns containing fans that force heat air through the leaves. After curing, the bright and yellow tobacco leaves are taken from the barns.

Before 2004, tobacco was sold at warehouse auctions in burlap sheets that contained up to 275 pounds of cured leaf. Since 2004, when Congress agreed to allow United States tobacco companies to buy out tobacco quota holders, tobacco has been placed in large 750-pound bales and delivered to warehouses, where tobacco companies have contracted with growers to grow and deliver cured leaf for the companies to purchase.

Tobacco has a three-hundred-year heritage and is a mainstay in the life and economy of South Carolina. Humid summers, hard work and pride in accomplishment combine to produce some of the world's finest tobacco.

SOUTH CAROLINA'S OTHER COMMODITIES

In 2007, South Carolina's agriculture industry adopted a marketing slogan to promote South Carolina agricultural products: "Nothing's Fresher. Nothing's Finer." The abundance and diversity of agricultural commodities produced in South Carolina inspired the slogan and it represents well the state's farmers' and producers' dedication to providing only the highest-quality products.

In addition to the more visible or individually profitable commodities highlighted on the previous pages, there are numerous other crops that add to South Carolina's flavor and fame and that are just as important. While they might not have the highest rankings in terms of overall sales, they are no less vital to the state's economy or no less important to consumers in the state and beyond. The United States Department of Agriculture's Agricultural Statistics Office refers to these valuable commodities as "Other Crops and Other Livestock" in its rankings. To the farmers who produce or raise these crops and animals and to the end users, they are every bit as representative of South Carolina agriculture as the more visible commodities. And to residents and tourists alike, many of these crops are representative and symbolic of South Carolina.

These various crops include peanuts, hay, oats, wheat, vegetables, sweet potatoes, peaches, pecans, apples, other fruits and nuts, tea, mi-

Larry Kemmerlin, a photographer for the Promotion and Education Division of the South Carolina Farm Bureau Federation, captured a close-up view of a head of wheat.

nor seed crops, miscellaneous field crops, and forest products. The additional livestock list includes chickens, hogs, other poultry, sheep and wool and goats and goats' milk. The category of "other" is rounded out with the unique products of aquaculture, honey and beeswax, horses, lambs and the all-encompassing word "miscellaneous," indicating that there is still more produced from South Carolina's rich soils and vibrant waters.

No discussion of renewable commodities and resources in South Carolina would be complete without acknowledging the impact and benefits of forestry. A 2006 study prepared for the Palmetto Agribusiness Council of South Carolina identified forestry as "an industry that impacts every corner of the state and plays an important role in every county's natural resource base." The report stated,

> *Forests cover two-thirds of South Carolina's total land area. They provide clean air and water, wildlife habitat, recreation and natural beauty, as well as a renewable forest products industry. Forests are essential to the state's economy, the environment, open space, and overall quality of life. The impact of forest products (forestry, logging, primary wood products and furniture manufacturing) on South Carolina's economy is over $17 billion annually and ranks second in value-added goods among the state's manufacturing sector.*

Indeed, South Carolina is blessed with an abundance and diversity of commodities. Citizens from all around the state submitted photographs depicting this variety and bounty. These photographs testify to the truth of the industry slogan. There is no doubt about it—when it comes to South Carolina agricultural products, "Nothing's Fresher. Nothing's Finer"!

Harvested pines being stacked using a front-end loader. Photo courtesy of Minnie Miller.

The impact of forest products (forestry, logging, primary wood products and furniture manufacturing) on South Carolina's economy is over seventeen billion dollars annually. Photograph by Larry Kemmerlin, South Carolina Farm Bureau Federation.

Peanuts—boiled, roasted, baked in a pie, salted or unsalted—are a South Carolina staple. Photograph by Minnie Miller.

A roadside produce stand in Bamberg County features fresh-picked, sun-ripened tomatoes and local watermelon. Photograph by Minnie Miller.

Mrs. Dori Sanders is the author of Dori Sanders' Country Cooking. *Here her brother, Orestu, picks greens near the Sanders' farm stand in York County. Photograph and information contributed by Clemson University professor Kenneth L. Robinson.*

The biosystems engineering program at Clemson University is a science-based engineering discipline that integrates engineering science and design with applied biological, biochemical and environmental sciences.

STATE AND NATIONAL ORGANIZATIONS

CLEMSON UNIVERSITY'S AGRICULTURAL HERITAGE

When one man of wisdom and foresight looks beyond the despair of troubled times and imagines what could be, great things can happen. That is what Clemson University's founder, Thomas Green Clemson, was able to do in the post-Civil War days. He looked upon a South that lay in economic ruin, once remarking that "conditions are wretched in the extreme," and that "people are quitting the land." Still, among the ashes he saw hope. Joined by his wife, Anna Calhoun Clemson, Mr. Clemson envisioned what could be possible if the South's youth were given an opportunity to receive instruction in scientific agriculture and the mechanical arts. He once wrote, "The only hope we have for the advancement of agriculture [in the United States] is through the sciences, and yet there is not one single institution on this continent where a proper scientific education can be obtained." When he was president of the Pendleton Farmers Society in 1866, Mr. Clemson served on a committee whose purpose was to promote the idea of founding an institution for "educating the people in the sciences" and "which will in time secure permanent prosperity."

When Clemson died on April 6, 1888, a series of events was set into motion that marked the start of a new era in higher education in South Carolina, especially in the study of science, agriculture and engineering. Mr. Clemson's passing set the stage for the founding of the university that bears his name—the beginning of a true "people's university," which opened the doors of higher education to all South Carolinians, rich and poor alike. In his will, which was signed November 6, 1886, Mr. Clemson bequeathed the Fort Hill plantation and a considerable sum from his personal assets for the establishment of an educational institution of the kind he envisioned. He left a cash endowment of approximately eighty thousand dollars and the 814-acre Fort Hill estate to South Carolina for such a college. The biggest obstacle in the creation of an agricultural college—the initial expense—was removed by Mr. Clemson's bequest.

On November 27, 1889, Governor Richardson signed the bill accepting Thomas Clemson's gift. Soon after, a measure was introduced to establish the Clemson Agricultural College, with its trustees becoming custodians of Morrill Act and Hatch Act funds made available for agricultural education and research by federal legislative acts. The founding of Clemson Agricultural College supplanted the South Carolina College of Agriculture and Mechanics, which had been designated in Columbia in 1880.

Born in Philadelphia, Mr. Clemson was educated at schools both in the United States and France, where he attended lectures at the Royal School of Mines, studied with prominent scientists in the private laboratories of the Sorbonne Royal College of France and received his diploma as an assayer from the Royal Mint in Paris. Mr. Clemson, then in his mid-twenties, returned to America greatly influenced by his European studies. He became a great advocate of the natural sciences, achieving a considerable reputation as a mining engineer and a theorist in agricultural chemistry. He also was a gifted writer whose articles were published in the leading scientific journals of his day, an artist and a diplomat who represented the U.S. government as chargé d'affaires to Belgium for almost seven years. He came to the foothills of South Carolina when he married Anna Maria Calhoun, daughter of South Carolina's famous statesman John C. Calhoun.

Mr. Clemson had a lifelong interest in farming and agricultural affairs. He served as the nation's first superintendent of agricultural affairs (predecessor to the present secretary of agriculture position) and actively promoted the establishment and endowment of the Maryland Agricultural College in the 1850s. Though remembered today for these accomplishments, Thomas Clemson made his greatest historical contribution when, as a champion of formal scientific education, his life became intertwined with the destiny of educational and economic development in South Carolina.

Thomas Green Clemson (July 1, 1807–April 6, 1888) is recognized as the benefactor and founder of Clemson University. In the days following the Civil War, he envisioned what would be possible if the South's youth were given an opportunity to receive instruction in scientific agriculture and the mechanical arts and upon his death, bequeathed enough land and money to the state for the establishment of an agricultural college. Thomas Green Clemson once wrote, "The only hope we have for the advancement of agriculture [in the United States] is through the sciences, and yet there is not one single institution on this continent where a proper scientific education can be obtained."

Dr. Scott Whiteside, a faculty member in Clemson's Department of Packaging Science, discusses the package designs of various products with a group.

Located in the Hendrix Student Center, the '55 Exchange is a student-run enterprise that manufactures, sells and serves Clemson's world-famous ice cream and other Clemson products like blue cheese and eggs. The '55 Exchange was made possible by a gift from the Class of 1955 and all revenues generated through this entrepreneurial center go to support Clemson students and their academic training.

The field of horticulture encompasses plant and vegetable physiology, pomology, cultural systems and germplasm enhancement, landscape architecture, pest management, molecular genetics, turfgrass management and physiology. The work of Clemson's faculty, staff and students fosters environmental stewardship while improving economic well-being, health and quality of life for all.

Although he never lived to see it, his dedicated efforts culminated in the founding of Clemson Agricultural College.

At the time of his death, Mr. Clemson was living at the Fort Hill homeplace, which today is a national historic landmark and provides a historic centerpiece for the Clemson University campus. He had inherited the house and plantation lands of his famous father-in-law, Senator John C. Calhoun, upon the death of Mrs. Clemson in 1875.

Clemson College formally opened in July 1893, with an enrollment of 446. From the beginning, the college was an all-male military school. It remained this way until 1955, when the change was made to "civilian" status for students and Clemson became a co-educational institution. In 1964, the college was renamed Clemson University as the state legislature formally recognized the school's expanded academic offerings and research pursuits. On November 27, 1989, the University observed the one hundredth anniversary of the State's acceptance of the terms and conditions of Mr. Clemson's bequest.

Today, the College of Agriculture, Forestry and Life Sciences (CAFLS) prepares students to cope with the global issues of the future and continues Thomas Green Clemson's dream of instructing young people in the agricultural and mechanical arts. Likewise, the research and outreach missions of the college extend through the University and the State to make discoveries and share knowledge. The ability of those in the College to understand and manipulate the molecular structures of biological systems offers immense potential to improve the world, whether that improvement is focused on foods, building products, the environment or the practice of medicine. CAFLS graduates currently employ their education and training in a wide variety of fields and endeavors.

Examples include producing more food on a planet whose farmlands are decreasing steadily; designing product packaging that is environmentally sound; growing better, healthier foods that prevent heart disease and other diseases; fighting breast cancer through medical research and practice; increasing dairy production and timber production; providing new fuel sources; and developing businesses that promote a "green" society.

Clemson's CAFLS is the *new* College of Agriculture, Forestry and Life Sciences. It blends a rich agricultural heritage with the miracles of the modern life sciences and produces graduates who contribute their talents and experience throughout the state, the country and even the world. CAFLS continues to develop strategic partnerships for the future, while maintaining its historical commitment to making the world happier, healthier, tastier and greener—and to fulfilling the original mission of Thomas Green Clemson.

SOUTH CAROLINA FARM BUREAU FEDERATION

South Carolina Farm Bureau began as an idea in the minds of a handful of progressive farmers seeking ways to improve the agricultural situation in the state during and after World War II.

On April 19, 1944, the State of South Carolina officially chartered the organization. Its purpose was "to effectively organize, advance, and improve, in every way possible, the agricultural interests of the State of South Carolina, economically, educationally and socially, through the united efforts of the county Farm Bureaus of the state." Robert R. Coker of Hartsville was elected as SCFB's first president.

After only a decade, SCFB had become a viable organization with more than twenty thousand members. During the 1950s, under the leadership of its second president, E. H. Agnew of Anderson County, the organization began to add member services—including an insurance program.

In November of 1962, SCFB started construction of an office building in Cayce, a location that continues to serve as the home office today. During the 1960s, the organization also added a number of service pro-

The Animal and Veterinary Sciences Department has been a part of Clemson's agricultural program since the early 1900s. The curriculum in AVS provides students with a broad understanding of scientific principles and the application of those principles to the scientific, technical and business phases of livestock and poultry production, processing and marketing. Hands-on instruction is emphasized and students are given many opportunities to work with animals.

The first South Carolina Farm Bureau Board of Directors pictured here in 1944.

Young farmers meet at the State House.

grams, such as the SCFB Marketing Association and the SCFB Services Corporation. David H. Sloan of Marion County served as SCFB's third president.

In 1971, the organization elected its fourth president, Harry S. Bell of Saluda County. Bell served as president of the organization for twenty-six years, a period during which membership more than tripled to more than one hundred thousand members. During this period, Bell also served as vice president of the American Farm Bureau Federation for eight years.

In December of 1997 at the annual meeting of the South Carolina Farm Bureau Federation, voting delegates elected Sumter County farmer David Winkles as the fifth president of the organization—a position he presently holds. Under his leadership, the Federation continues to flourish and serves as the voice of agriculture in South Carolina, helping to keep family farmers in business and rural lifestyles thriving. Winkles also serves on the American Farm Bureau Federation Board of Directors and he is a prominent witness and spokesman on the issues of international agricultural trade and the benefits of biotechnology on the farm.

The South Carolina Farm Bureau continues to be a general farm organization with county chapters open for membership to anyone who recognizes the value of locally produced food, fiber and fuel. Anyone who values the work and worth of family farmers, rural lifestyles and locally grown commodities is invited by the South Carolina Farm Bureau to attend a county chapter meeting anytime.

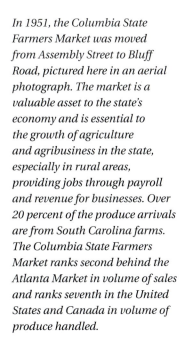

In 1951, the Columbia State Farmers Market was moved from Assembly Street to Bluff Road, pictured here in an aerial photograph. The market is a valuable asset to the state's economy and is essential to the growth of agriculture and agribusiness in the state, especially in rural areas, providing jobs through payroll and revenue for businesses. Over 20 percent of the produce arrivals are from South Carolina farms. The Columbia State Farmers Market ranks second behind the Atlanta Market in volume of sales and ranks seventh in the United States and Canada in volume of produce handled.

SOUTH CAROLINA DEPARTMENT OF AGRICULTURE

The year was 1879. Governor Wade Hampton resigned to become a United States senator. Thomas Edison demonstrated the electric light. Milk was sold in bottles for the first time. A refrigeration apparatus was patented. And the Office of the Commissioner of Agriculture and the South Carolina Department of Agriculture were established by Legislative Act on December 23 of that year.

At that time, the department was responsible for statistics, labor, immigration, manufacturing and industry, real estate and mining. The department also supervised fishing interests, quarantined contagious animals and enforced seed regulations and commercial fertilizer. By law, all fertilizer manufacturers were required to pay twenty-five cents per ton of fertilizer or commercial manure sold. Due to the economic stress on the state from the aftermath of the Civil War, Clemson College assumed some of the department's responsibilities in 1890, including the regulation of fertilizers. The department ceased to operate as a separate entity until March 15, 1904, when an act re-established the South Carolina Department of Agriculture, Commerce and Immigration. Two thousand dollars was appropriated for operating the department. There have been ten commissioners of agriculture since 1904 serving South Carolina in that capacity.

Pictured here is the farmers market constructed between 1935 and 1936 on Assembly Street with the assistance of Roosevelt's New Deal Works Progress Administration (WPA). The concrete median of this market remains today, symbolizing the market's historical presence.

The original Act of 1904 called for the commissioner to have "the qualifications of a good moral character and a competent knowledge of matters of immigration, manufacturing, publicity and general industries." He was charged with "the promotion of agriculture, manufacturing and other industries, cattle raising, and all matters tending to the industrial development of the state." He was to collect and publish "information relative to the advantages of soil and climate and to the natural resources and industrial opportunities offered in the state," and to publish a land registry. He was also to publish a handbook of the state containing "information designed to attract people to South Carolina."

The *South Carolina Market Bulletin* was first published in the summer of 1913 when the department was established as a bureau of marketing through which farmers could list produce they had for sale and people could send in lists of items wanted. Except for a brief period in the depths of the Depression, the *Bulletin* has been published continuously. The *Market Bulletin* now reaches thousands of farm and non-farm families who buy and sell agricultural-related items.

After years of research and planning, the Columbia State Farmers Market is now in its fifth renaissance. The new State Farmers Market, located on 213 acres on Highway 321 in Lexington County near Dixiana, blends the character of markets past with the latest innovations to meet the expectations of twenty-first-century consumers.

The Columbia State Farmers Market became a part of the South Carolina Department of Agriculture in 1975. Later, the Greenville State Farmers Market came under the direction of the department, and in 1989 the Pee Dee Farmers Market, located between Florence and Darlington, was established.

The State Warehouse System, which allows farmers to store cotton and grain and take a receipt for the storage that can be used to borrow money from lending institutions, was added to the department's duties over fifty years ago.

In all, about thirty-seven separate laws have been passed and assigned to the department. Each of the department's divisions is headed by a director who manages specialists within each function. Program areas include agricultural services, consumer services and laboratory services.

Today, the South Carolina Department of Agriculture continues to serve farmers and non-farmers, producers and consumers. Agriculture is no longer just a means for sustenance as it was before 1879. It's also a vital part of the state's economic well-being, and while assuring the safety and security of the buying public, the Department of Agriculture plays an essential role in nurturing that economic growth and development.

THE UNITED STATES DEPARTMENT OF AGRICULTURE

The United States Department of Agriculture (USDA) was officially established during the Lincoln Administration in 1862 along with the Morrill Act, which promoted education, and the Homestead Act, which offered public land free to anyone who would farm it. Since the establishment of the department and these two initial pieces of legislation, numerous laws and policies have been passed throughout the last century to support agricultural producers, allied industries and most importantly the American consumer. The department is responsible for the administration of the majority of the government regulations that impact the farm from finance to statistics, trade and public consumption. Some of the better-known agencies include: Cooperative State Research, Education and Extension Service (CSREES), Farm Service Agency (FSA), Forest Service (FS), National Agricultural Statistics Service (NASS) and Natural Resources Conservation Service (NRCS). It is this last agency, NRCS, that has been integral in inspiring agriculturalists to be "keepers of the land" as they till the land for profit.

The Soil Conservation Service in South Carolina sponsored a float in the November 1935 Armistice Day Parade in Spartanburg.

A farmer plows a field in Spartanburg in 1937.

A group of Boiling Springs High School science and geography students learn about kudzu and its use in soil defense on steep and eroded slopes.

The Natural Resources Conservation Service (NRCS), part of the United States Department of Agriculture (USDA), draws on a tradition of principles in working with private landowners that is as relevant today as when it was a dream to Hugh Hammond Bennett in the late 1920s and early 1930s. A career soil scientist in the USDA, Bennett became convinced that soil erosion was a national menace and that the solution lay in tailoring conservation practices to fit the capability of the land and the desires of landowners. He felt that attempting to find simple solu-

tions that were applied to all situations would be fruitless—a one-size-fits-all solution would not work. Crops, land and climates were so diverse from one region to another that specialists in agronomy, forestry, soil science, biology, engineering and social sciences would need to work with local farmers to find conservation solutions and methods that would benefit the land and fulfill landowners' aspirations.

In 1933, the Soil Erosion Service, predecessor to the Soil Conservation Service and NRCS, began working with farmers in the Coon Creek watershed of southwestern Wisconsin to transform the square, eroding fields into what is seen today—a conservation showplace of contouring, strip-cropping, terracing and wise land use that benefits the soil, air and water, as well as the plants, animals and people of the whole watershed.

The passage of the Soil Conservation Act in April of 1935 hastened the nationwide implementation of soil conservation practices. Recognition of the first conservation district, bounded by the Brown Creek watershed in North Carolina, on August 4, 1937, established a method for the Soil

Erosion Service to assist farmers in the conservation districts. Locally elected citizens established priorities and plans for the district's work.

The four original principles of NRCS still guide its work today: (1) Assess the resources on the land, the conservation problems and the opportunities; (2) Draw on various sciences and disciplines and integrate all their contributions into a plan for the whole property; (3) Work closely with land users so the plans for conservation mesh with their objectives; and (4) Through implementing conservation on individual properties, contribute to the overall quality of life in the watershed or region.

With the mission of "Helping People Help the Land," the Natural Resources Conservation Service (NRCS) in South Carolina provides products and services that enable people to be good stewards of the state's and the nation's soil, water and related natural resources on non-federal lands. With the help of NRCS, people are better able to conserve, maintain or improve their natural resources. As a result of the technical and financial assistance provided by NRCS, land managers and communities are able to take a comprehensive approach to the use and protection of natural resources in rural, suburban, urban and developing areas.

NRCS reaches out to all segments of the agricultural community, including underserved and socially disadvantaged farmers and ranchers, to ensure that its programs and services are accessible to everyone.

NATIONAL FFA ORGANIZATION

Much of the historical information for this article was provided by Dr. Philip M. Fravel, a member of the faculty in the Agricultural Education Program at Clemson University.

The South Carolina Future Farmers of America Association (FFA) began in October 1927, when a group of agricultural education students from some one hundred high schools throughout the state met during the third week of October at the South Carolina State Fair in Columbia. The purpose of their gathering was to organize what was known then as the Future Palmetto Farmers. It was modeled after the Virginia plan of 1926, which was the forerunner of the National Future Farmers of America. The South Carolina organization later became a charter member of the National FFA, which was established in 1928. Palmetto Farmers became the fifth state group to assume the name of the national group and became known as the South Carolina Association of Future Farmers of America.

FFA members and agriculture teacher Joe Wilson present poinsettias to Clemson University President Jim Barker on behalf of the Aiken County Future Farmers of America.

In 1988, the name of the Agricultural Education student group was changed to the National FFA Organization to better reflect the expanded number of professional careers available to its members. As South Carolina entered the twenty-first century, there were more than three

FFA members attend an FFA Legislative Day address on the steps of the Capitol in Columbia.

hundred career opportunities available in the science, business and technology of agriculture. Farming, the primary career when the FFA was organized, continues to be one of the most important and rewarding of those numerous careers.

The FFA is an integral, intra-curricular part of agricultural education as outlined by Public Law 740, which provides the FFA a federal charter. The FFA operates at the local, state and national levels and is organized by school chapters with teachers serving as chapter advisors.

The National FFA Organization has a paid membership of more than five hundred thousand students from more than 7,300 chapters in all fifty states, Puerto Rico and the Virgin Islands. The membership is about equally divided between rural farm, rural non-farm, urban and suburban areas. Approximately 40 percent of the FFA membership is female and females hold more than 50 percent of the leadership positions in the organization at the local, state and national levels.

FFA members in South Carolina and the nation have an opportunity to learn career skills and participate in more than forty-five national proficiency areas through hands-on experience. Proficiency areas range from food science and technology to turfgrass management to wildlife production and management to many areas in production agriculture. Members may also compete in some twenty-three national career development events in categories such as public speaking, environmental and natural resources, agronomy, farm business management, dairy foods and nursery and landscape design.

The South Carolina FFA Association manages the South Carolina FFA Center in North Myrtle Beach. The property was purchased by FFA members in 1956 and has operated since 1959, affording many students their first glimpse of the Atlantic Ocean in addition to providing educational and leadership activities and opportunities. In 2000, the FFA Foundation contributed one million dollars

In 2004, Clemson University's Center for Apparel Research designed the new National FFA jacket.

S. F. Horton of Loris, a native of Chesterfield County and a Clemson University graduate in Agricultural Education, was a delegate to the organizational meeting of the Future Palmetto Farmers at the State Fair in Columbia in October of 1927.

to fund improvements to the center, which included the renovation of many of its dormitories.

The South Carolina FFA Association has promoted its work through a member magazine for many years. In the early 2000s, John W. Parris, head of the association's Office of Public Affairs, led the effort to revise the magazine and *AgriBiz* debuted. Published quarterly, the magazine reports chapter, state and national activities and features educational, informational and other articles of interest, along with student success stories.

Clemson University has been an active partner with South Carolina FFA for many years. The leadership for Agricultural Education was transferred from the State Department of Education to Clemson University in 1996. Since then, Clemson has devoted staff and resources to assist with FFA activities and provide in-service training to develop and support FFA chapters throughout the state.

Clemson University has also impacted the National FFA Organization. In 2004, Clemson's Center for Apparel Research designed the new National FFA jacket. Students from the Anderson, Blue Ridge, Travelers Rest and West Oak FFA chapters served as fit models at each stage of the redesign project.

The mission of the FFA is to make a positive difference in the lives of students by developing their potential for premier leadership, personal growth and career success through agricultural education. The FFA's motto, "Learning to Do, Doing to Learn, Earning to Live and Living to Serve," continues to inspire students to reach for the stars in their quest for excellence in agricultural education.

SOUTH CAROLINA 4-H: MAKING THE BEST BETTER SINCE 1907

A movement began in the early 1900s through the United States Department of Agriculture (USDA) to use the Land Grant College System to train and educate young people in the best techniques available for success in agriculture. The USDA leaders reasoned that progress and change in agriculture would occur more rapidly if youth were trained, so youth agriculture clubs were established. Today, the South Carolina 4-H Youth Development Program uses a learn-by-doing approach, the involvement of caring adults and the knowledge and resources of Clemson University and the land grant university system to empower youth to become healthy, productive and caring members of society.

Two 4-H students, in their signature green-colored jackets, deliver a speech.

In 1908, A. L. Easterling, superintendent of schools in Marlboro County, organized the first Boy's Corn Club. In 1910, Miss Marie Cromer, an Aiken County schoolteacher, organized the first Girls' Tomato Canning Club. These clubs were the forerunners of the 4-H clubs in South Carolina. Teaching others and becoming involved in the community were part of the missions of these early clubs,

149

and are still major expectations for 4-H club members. Today, 4-H is defined as "a community of young people across America who are learning leadership, citizenship and life skills."

In 1911, Mrs. Dora D. "Mother" Walker was appointed County Tomato Club Agent in Barnwell County. She became the first county home demonstration agent in the world. Today, almost every county in South Carolina has a Clemson University 4-H agent to organize and implement positive youth development programs and activities. In addition, hundreds of trained 4-H volunteers work in partnership with youth through a variety of 4-H projects in agriculture, animal science, natural resources, technology, engineering, healthy lifestyles, leadership, citizenship and personal development.

By the early 1920s, the youth education program was recognized nationally as 4-H, and had adopted the well-known cloverleaf emblem symbolizing Head, Heart, Hands and Health.

• HEAD: Youth develop managing and thinking skills. The 4-H projects involve youth in planning, organizing, goal-setting and decision-making. This teaches them wise use of resources, record keeping, problem solving and resiliency.

• HEART: Youth develop relating and caring skills. The 4-H projects involve youth in social skills, cooperation and conflict resolution. This teaches them concern for others, empathy, accepting differences and communication.

Chester County has a long history of youth participation in 4-H livestock projects. Chester County Calf Club members display their banner at the 1928 South Carolina State Fair. Photograph and information contributed by Robin Currence.

J. G. Grant Jr., a 4-H member from Chester County, raised prize-winning corn and exhibited it at the South Carolina State Fair in 1928. Photograph and information contributed by Robin Currence.

• HANDS: Youth develop giving and working skills. The 4-H projects involve youth in responsible citizenship, community service and teamwork. This teaches them leadership, self-motivation and marketable skills.

• HEALTH: Youth develop living and being skills. The 4-H projects involve youth in healthy lifestyle choices, disease prevention and personal safety. This teaches them character, responsibility, self-esteem, self-discipline and stress management.

As part of the largest youth organization in the country, today's 4-H program serves thousands of South Carolina youth ages five to nineteen. South Carolina's 4-H program has been run by the Cooperative Extension Service at Clemson University since 1914.

The 4-H Motto: To Make the Best Better.
The 4-H Slogan: Learn By Doing.
The 4-H Pledge: I pledge my Head to clearer thinking, my Heart to greater loyalty, my Hands to larger service, and my Health to better living, for my club, my community, my country and my world.

Four-year-old Chance Hare (left) and his brother, Colton Hare, pose with their Australian Shepard, Gus, at their uncle's farm in Westminster. Photograph contributed by Crystal Hare.

THE FUTURE OF AGRICULTURE

When we began soliciting photographs for *Barns, Barbecue and Bales of Cotton*, we spread the word near and far to the citizens of South Carolina, asking them to share photographs of rural farm structures including old and new barns, tobacco barns and animal housing, just to name a few; snapshots of classic rural social gatherings like church meetings, family holidays and reunions, pig-pickin's, Lowcountry seafood boils, hunting excursions or any joyous rural South Carolina gathering featuring food, fun and fellowship; and photos depicting the rich heritage of South Carolina agricultural production from field to market including animals, eggs, milk, cotton, tobacco, grains, peaches and the like.

When I excitedly opened the first group of five envelopes, I was surprised. In three of the envelopes were beautiful, professional photographs of adorable children dressed in rural attire and posed in picturesque agricultural and rural settings. I felt a moment of panic and thought, "Oh no, did we somehow ask for people to send in photos of their children and grandchildren in agricultural regalia?" I immediately grabbed one of our submission forms and scanned it from top to bottom, front and back. There was not one word regarding photos of young people enjoying the pleasures of rural life. I was relieved, and reasoned that these photographs were simply from thoughtful friends of the college sharing favorite photographs of their dear children or grandchildren.

As time progressed and photo after photo of adorable children arrived in the mail, however, I realized that what these citizens were sharing was "the future of agriculture" in South Carolina. Their photographs represented the hopes and dreams of agriculturalists from the greatest generation and the baby boomer generation, who are seeking to share their love of agriculture and rural life with the next generation.

Once I and the others involved with the production of the book realized this, we felt compelled to include a representative collage of some of these photos. Unfortunately, there was not space enough to showcase them all, but it is inspiring to know that the smiling faces of these young people represent countless others, who are each day developing and cultivating a fondness and passion for South Carolina's rural way of life and for the agricultural economy that sustains this life. As we in the College of Agriculture, Forestry and Life Sciences say, "May their tribe increase— what we need now more than ever are young people who are willing to be agriculture's *new* professionals!"

Siblings Kate (five years old), Clair (two years old) and Bowen (one month old) stand in an Aiken cotton field, near where their father, Stephen Bright Jr., grew up. Their mother, Rosalind Bright, had always admired the beauty of this field. When she learned it was to be sold and re-zoned for commercial development, she photographed her children among the snowy white cotton as a means of immortalizing the field for her family. Rosalind Bright graduated from Clemson University in 1999.

Young gardeners Emily (left) and Hope Spencer from Bamberg County like to pitch in with chores around the farm. Photograph by Minnie Miller.

Five-year-old Leah proudly shows off her hand-painted sign in Williamston. She has helped her Papa, Charles Mauldin, pick tomatoes and ready them for sale. Photograph contributed by Sandra Edens of Belton.

Ten-year-old Amber Mincey and her one-and-a-half-year-old brother, Christian, show off their pet duck, Quackers, on their family's farm in Nichols. Photograph contributed by Debra Mincey.

Ben Palecek surveys a cotton field at a York County farm operated by Darby Farms. Photograph contributed by Harriet Palecek.

During a summer visit to the Pageland home of his grandparents, W. K. and Lisa Oliver, Caleb Smith took an interest in his grandfather's push plow. Photograph contributed by Lisa Oliver.

Grace Moore smiles from the side of a catch pen owned by James Henry Bledsoe located in Saluda as her parents and others "worked cows." Photograph contributed by Leigh Moore.

Children's book author Beth Reynolds holds a baby goat for two budding farmers to pet on Papa Bruce's Barnyard in Piedmont. Photograph contributed by Bruce Hokombe.

Riding the tractor is just one of the many activities Bryson Paul Simmons delights in when he visits his Uncle Craig and Aunt Mei Mei on their farm in Wedgefield. Photograph contributed by Kay Simmons.

Brayden Couch loves tractors and was excited to work this cotton "snowball" field in Honea Path. Photograph contributed by Lisa Phillips Couch.

A young 4-H member learns about the history of the railroad in South Carolina at the Rivers, Rails and Crossroads Discovery Center located on the campus of the Edisto REC in Blackville. Photograph by Minnie Miller.

Keith Coker and his grandson, Cory, ride the tractor in the pasture of his Gray Court residence. Cory is learning that living in the country and owning animals is a lot of work. Photograph contributed by Betty Coker.

Young beekeeper Anona Miller suits up to help her father work the family's beehives in Bamberg County. As the beekeeping population ages, young people are encouraged to learn the trade. Photograph by Minnie Miller.

Jessica, the five-year-old niece of Sandra Edens, loves to dip and sip the cool water from the well at Aunt Sandra's Cheddar Community home in Belton. Photograph provided by Sandra Edens.

RESOURCE GUIDE

SOUTH CAROLINA AGENCIES

South Carolina Department of Agriculture
P.O. Box 11280, 1200 Senate Street, Columbia, SC 29211
Phone: 803-734-2210—http://agriculture.sc.gov/

South Carolina State Climatology Office—
http://water.dnr.state.sc.us/climate/sco/index

South Carolina Department of Health and Environmental Control—
www.scdhec.net

South Carolina Forestry Commission—www.state.sc.us/forest

South Carolina Rural Development Council—www.state.sc.us/scrdc

AGRICULTURAL ASSOCIATIONS AND BOARDS

Up-to-date contact information for many associations and boards is available at the SC Department of Agriculture's website—http://agriculture.sc.gov/—under the Resources Tab.

SOUTH CAROLINA COMMODITY BOARDS

South Carolina Cattle and Beef Board

South Carolina Cotton Board

South Carolina Peanut Board

South Carolina Pork Board

South Carolina Soybean Board

South Carolina Tobacco Board

South Carolina Watermelon Board

SOUTH CAROLINA AGRICULTURE ASSOCIATIONS

South Carolina Apple Growers Association

South Carolina Aquaculture Association

South Carolina Beekeepers Association—
http://www.scstatebeekeepers.org/

South Carolina Cattlemen's Association—www.sccattle.org

South Carolina Christmas Tree Growers' Association—
www.scchristmastrees.org

South Carolina Corn and Soybean Association—www.scsoybeans.org

South Carolina Dairy Association—www.midnet.sc.edu/scda/

South Carolina Fruit/Vegetable Specialty Crop Association

South Carolina Horsemen's Council—www.schorsecouncil.org

South Carolina Landscape and Turfgrass Association—www.sclta.com

South Carolina Livestock Markets Association

South Carolina Meat Goat Association—www.scmga.tripod.com

South Carolina Nursery and Landscape Association—www.scnla.com

South Carolina Peach Council—
http://www.scpeach.com/museum.htm

South Carolina Poultry Federation

South Carolina Seafood Alliance—http://www.scseafood.org

South Carolina Seedmen's Association

South Carolina Sheep Industries Association

South Carolina Specialty Food Association—http://www.scsfa.org/

South Carolina Tobacco Growers' Association

South Carolina Tomato Association

South Carolina Watermelon Association

South Carolina Farm Bureau Federation
724 Knox Abbott Dr, Cayce, SC, 29033-3340, Phone:
1-866-FB-MEMBER—www.scfb.org

South Carolina Fertilizer and Agrichemical Association—
www.scfaa.org

South Carolina Forestry Association—www.scforestry.org

CLEMSON UNIVERSITY

College of Agriculture, Forestry and Life Sciences
101 Barre Hall, Clemson University, Clemson, SC 29634,
Phone: 864-656-3010—www.clemson.edu/cafls

Clemson University Cooperative Extension Service—
www.clemson.edu/extension

Clemson University Public Service—
http://www.clemson.edu/public/

Coastal Research & Education Center—
www.clemson.edu/coastalrec

Edisto Research & Education Center—
www.clemson.edu/edisto

Pee Dee Research & Education Center—
www.clemson.edu/peedeerec

Sandhill Research & Education Center—
www.clemson.edu/agforestryresearch/sandhill.htm

NATIONAL GOVERNMENT AGENCIES

United States Department of Agriculture—www.usda.gov

Divisions

National Agricultural Statistics Service—www.usda.gov/nass

South Carolina, National Agricultural Statistics Service—
www.nass.usda.gov/sc

Economic Research Service—www.ers.usda.gov

Farm Service Agency—www.fsa.usda.gov

Forestry Service—www.state.sc.us/forest

Joint Agricultural Weather Facility—
www.usda.gov/oce/waob/jawf

Natural Resources Conservation Service—
www.nrcs.usda.gov

South Carolina, Natural Resources Conservation Service—
www.sc.nrcs.usda.gov

National Agricultural Library—www.nal.usda.gov

Risk Management Agency—www.rma.usda.gov

OTHER

South Carolina State University Extension—www.scsu.edu

National FFA Online—www.ffa.org

National 4-H Online—http://www.4husa.org

Canadian Agriculture Statistics—www.statcan.ca

AgFirst Farm Credit Bank—www.agfirst.com

ArborOne Farm Credit Bank—http://www.arborone.com

South Carolina Barbeque Association—www.scbarbeque.com

ABOUT THE CONTRIBUTORS

Rowland P. Alston Jr., Clemson University County Extension agent emeritus, served as an Extension agent for nearly thirty years in Sumter, South Carolina. In addition to his usual duties, Rowland became associated with public broadcasting in the early 1980s, and in 1993 was a co-creator of the Emmy Award-winning South Carolina ETV show *Making it Grow!* A live, interactive call-in program produced by ETV and Clemson University, *Making it Grow!* brings viewers current, research-based horticultural information. As host, Rowland, along with featured guests, focuses on gardening topics while highlighting interesting places and products from around South Carolina.

Rowland holds a Bachelor of Science in Agricultural Education and a master's degree in agronomy, both from Clemson University. He resides in the Rembert Community of Sumter County, South Carolina, with his wife Martha. When he's not working with *Making it Grow!*, he can usually be found sitting on a John Deere tractor or deep-sea fishing.

Dr. Walter Edgar was born and reared in Mobile, Alabama. He received his Bachelor of Arts from Davidson College and his Master of Arts and Doctor of Philosophy from the University of South Carolina. After serving in the Army for two years, he returned to USC in 1972 and joined the History Department after completing a fellowship. He founded and served as the first director of the History Department's acclaimed Public History Program. In 1980, he was named director of the Institute for Southern Studies.

During the more than three decades of his academic career, Dr. Edgar has written or edited more than a dozen books and has engaged in numerous other academic pursuits. Since 2000, he has been the host of two popular weekly programs heard statewide on South Carolina ETV–Radio: *Walter Edgar's Journal* and *Southern Read*.

His hobbies include reading, gardening and judging South Carolina barbecue.

Robert A. Graham Sr. owes his love for agriculture to his uncle and grandfather, who farmed together in Kewanee, Illinois. Bob holds a Bachelor of Science (1968) and a Master of Science (1969) in Agricultural Economics from Clemson University. He worked for the National Agricultural Statistics Service, a division of the United States Department of Agriculture, for thirty-seven years and served as director of the South Carolina office from 1994 until his retirement in January 2006.

In the closing years of his service for the National Agricultural Statistics Service, Bob led an initiative to collect photographs of old barns for the cover and layout of the *South Carolina Agricultural Statistics Census Report*. This activity earned him the nickname "Old Barn Bob."

Bob is a Vietnam veteran who resides in Lexington, South Carolina, with his wife Cindy. He works part-time for the Family Christian Store, is involved with many activities at his church and enjoys reading and listening to Bluegrass music.

Lake E. High Jr. was born in Columbia, South Carolina, and, except for a few years spent in Washington, D.C., has resided there all of his life. One of his earliest childhood memories is holding his father's hand and being taken to Lever's Barbeque restaurant, which was at the time in West Columbia. He loved it.

Lake's profession is that of a stockbroker. However, when he first graduated from the University of South Carolina with a major in political science, he worked in the public relations section of the South Carolina Electric Cooperatives Association. His position at the association gave him the opportunity to travel throughout the state for several days each week, eventually taking him to every county in South Carolina. As Lake traveled the state, he never missed a barbecue house. By the time he was twenty-seven or so, friends had begun urging him to write a book on South Carolina barbecue, given that he had probably eaten in more real barbecue restaurants than anyone else in South Carolina. He didn't write the book, but he is currently working on a Web site, which will list "The 100 Top Barbeque Houses in South Carolina." This list is probably the closest thing you'll find to that suggested book.

Before his venture into the field of judging barbecue, Lake was a certified wine judge. His twenty years of experience in that area gave him an excellent background in tasting and judging, a background that has been valuable in teaching others how to judge barbecue.

In 2004, Lake and Dr. Walter Rolandi founded the South Carolina Barbeque Association with the objective being to train other barbecue judges and help towns and organizations put on local barbecue festivals. In the first five years of the SCBA's existence, the organization helped start more than twenty-five different barbecue cook-offs and trained more than five hundred barbecue judges. Lake currently serves as the president of the SCBA and continually looks forward to his next plate of barbecue.

Kirby Player is a farm boy raised on a crop farm in Lee County in the rich agricultural Pee Dee region of South Carolina. He received a Bachelor of Science in Agricultural Education from Clemson University in 1983, and had the honor of serving as the student body president of Clemson University during the 1982–1983 academic year. While working in the food service industry from 1983–1987, Kirby completed a master's degree at Clemson in parks, recreation and tourism management with an emphasis in human resource development. He is currently pursuing a Ph.D. in Therapeutic Recreation with a focus on obesity and lifestyle change.

In February of 1989, Kirby was appointed coordinator of student relations and recruitment for the College of Agricultural Sciences at Clemson University. In 1996, that college merged with various Life Science and Natural Resource programs to become the College of Agriculture, Forestry and Life Sciences. In his twenty years with the college, Kirby has administered student, alumni and donor relations and public information.

Kirby resides in Clemson, South Carolina, with his wife Marilyn, and feels blessed every day when he goes to work because he believes "I have been blessed with a mission, not just a job!"

Endsheet photographs (front and back) by Brian Roberts.